Writer  Mama

How to Raise a Writing Career
Alongside Your Kids

CHRISTINA
KATZ

WRITER'S DIGEST BOOKS

www.writersdigest.com
Cincinnati, Ohio

Distributed in Canada by Fraser Direct, 100 Armstrong Avenue, Georgetown, ON, Canada L7G 5S4, Tel: (905) 877-4411. Distributed in the U.K. and Europe by David & Charles, Brunel House, Newton Abbot, Devon, TQ12 4PU, England, Tel: (+44) 1626 323200, Fax: (+44) 1626 323319, E-mail: postmaster@davidandcharles.co.uk. Distributed in Australia by Capricorn Link, P.O. Box 704, Windsor, NSW 2756 Australia, Tel: (02) 4577-3555.

Visit our Web site at www.writersdigest.com and www.wdeditors.com for information on more resources for writers.

To receive a free weekly e-mail newsletter delivering tips and updates about writing and about Writer's Digest products, register directly at our Web site at http://newsletters.fwpublications.com.

Pinted in Canada

11 10 09 08 07   5 4 3 2 1

Library of Congress Cataloging-in-Publication Data
Katz, Christina.
  Writer mama : how to raise a writing career alongside your kids / by Christina Katz. -- 1st edition.
      p. cm.
  Includes bibliographical references and index.
  ISBN-13: 978-1-58297-441-5 (pbk. : alk. paper)
  ISBN-10: 1-58297-441-1 (pbk. : alk. paper)
  1. Housewives as authors. 2. Authorship. 3. Authorship--Vocational guidance. I. Title.
PN171.H67K38 2007
808'.02--dc22
                    2006037357

Edited by Michelle Ehrhard and Jane Friedman
Designed by Claudean Wheeler
Cover Illustration by Paul Oakley
Production coordinated by Mark Griffin

F•W PUBLICATIONS, INC.

Dedication

This book is for writer mamas everywhere. May you find satisfaction and profits as a result of your writing-for-publication efforts!

And also for my husband, Jason, and my daughter, Samantha, who mean the world to me.

Acknowledgments

A village made it possible for me to write this book. Elaura Niles and Julie Fast helped uncover the idea. Jane Friedman and Michelle Ehrhard were instrumental in the book's direction and depth. Rita Rosenkranz brought her considerable professionalism and poise to the table. My students, past and present, inspired me. My husband, Jason, shouldered a lot of extra responsibilities so I could work extra hours. My daughter, Samantha, was consistently a delight, which certainly helped. Our childcare providers at Belinda's and play-date buddies, Barb and Jamie, were accommodating and dependable. Kristin O'Keeffe was the only one who could have seen me through drafts one through xxx (I lost count of how many somewhere along the way). Sage Cohen was a terrific cheerleader. The columnists at *Writers on the Rise* kept me going—a couple of them, Wendy Burt and Kelly James-Enger—have been great role models over the years. My grandmother, Amelia Perry, told great stories when I was a kid, which is how I caught the writing bug. My parents gave me the best education hard-earned money can buy, took me to the public library, and are voracious readers, which explains a lot. And finally, the power that moves me to write deserves credit. Thanks for helping me to embrace the ride as much as the results.

Table of Contents

Introduction: A Pep Talk 1

I. Preparation

1. Accumulate Ideas 9
   Idea-Keeping
2. Identify Your Audiences 19
   The Benefits of Freelancing
3. Tear Apart Target Markets 29
   Six Benefits of Being a Write-at-Home Mom
4. Digest the Guidelines 39
   Scrounge for an Hour in the A.M.
5. Tackle the Clips Catch-22 47
   Gather Every Afternoon Moment
6. Connect With Cover Letters 58
   Wring Every Second From the Evenings

II. Practice

7. Tip Off Everyone 69
   Stake Out Spaces and Start a Wishlist

8. List Your Way Into Print 79
   How to Handle Procrastination
9. Satisfy Editorial Needs With Fillers 89
   Streamline Household Management
10. Show Your Readers How It's Done 99
    Heroine Worship
11. Trumpet Your Personal Stories 108
    Practicing Good Boundaries
12. Become a Serial Specialist 119
    The Possibility of Childcare

III. Professionalism

13. Prewrite Your Feature 132
    Find Your Tribe—Live!
14. Draft Your Query 143
    Find Your Tribe—Online or Via E-Mail!
15. Plan for Query Success 155
    Uncover Your Beliefs About Editors
16. Go Get the Interviews 178
    Rolodex Power
17. Negotiate Like a Barter Queen 191
    Set Satisfaction-Based (and Monetary) Goals
18. Run With Your Assignment 204
    Writing Career Ups and Downs

IV. Poise

19. Wear All the Right Hats 217
    Seventeen Ways to Avoid Writer Mama Burnout
20. Establish Expertise in Your Field 230
    Imitate the Attitude of Writer Mama Pros
21. Get Your Name Known 245
    Develop Multiple Income Streams
22. Count Down Days to a Conference 257
    Be a Prepared Conference Attendee
23. Pitch a Nonfiction Book Concept 272
    How to Pitch a Book Concept

Afterword: There Is No End, Just More to Learn 282

Appendix: Recommended Reading 285

Index 288

About the Author 296

Introduction

A Pep Talk

> For both my jobs, as a mom and as a writer, I utilize creativity, time management, organizational skills, and patience. You don't need a M.F.A. from a fancy college to be a writer—if you're a mom, you already have most of the skills you need.
>
> ~ TIFFANY TALBOTT, MOTHER OF ONE

Motherhood and writing ... can they go together? Yes! In fact, for many moms, they already do. In the past, we didn't always know our favorite authors were moms. Today, it seems like everyone's talking about motherhood and writing, often in the same breath.

Whether you are about to have your first child or you already have children underfoot, the thought may have crossed your mind, "Is now a good time to launch a writing career?" Maybe you always wanted to write. Maybe you are staying home from your job for a short time. Or maybe writing occurred to you as a possible career you could do alongside mothering, in hopes of working at home full time in the near future.

Maybe you have been looking for a book that breaks down the myriad of decisions—Write first, or query first? Submit to local, regional, or national publications? Specialize or generalize?—into manageable steps. But you've never found the book that specifically addresses your desire to reach short-term goals quickly, while teaching you to think strategically about the future and steadily build a solid foundation for a long-term career.

This book will help you get published sooner, while still keeping an eye on your long-term writing goals and balancing your responsibilities at home. It's chock-full of experience and advice from moms who write both full and part time. And when you are ready to get your words into print, this book will help you practice the skills published writer mamas use to stay in print. In short, this book will help you "think" like a published writer mama and, therefore, you'll make more informed choices as you move along in your writing career.

So if you're a mom who feels called to write, should you heed the call? Absolutely. When I became a mom, that's when I stopped waiting to be "discovered" and took my career into my own already full hands. If you are still not

Have you dreamed of being a published writer—but you already have a fulltime job as a mom? Take heart—*Writer Mama* teaches you how to make the most of your limited time, educates you about the world of publishing, and gives you tips to help you boost your chances of success. Even the busiest mom will find ways to pursue and reach her writing dreams with this motivating, practical, tip-driven book.

Kelly James-Enger, books including *Six-Figure Freelancing: The Writer's Guide to Making More Money* (Random House, 2005)

Writer Mama is a solid, sensible guide that is sure to help any woman who wants to pursue a professional writing career while raising her children.

Eric Maisel, *Creativity for Life* (New World Library, 2007)

What a find! *Writer Mama* is a must for any woman beginning a freelance career. A combination of inspiration and practical information, this book offers solid guidelines and tips on how to make a living writing while raising a family.

Barbara DeMarco-Barrett, *Pen On Fire: A Busy Woman's Guide to Igniting the Writer Within* (Harcourt, 2004)

Sure to be a favorite among moms who need a little help sorting out the challenges of balancing family and career. Packed with practical advice in reader-friendly format.

Jenna Glatzer, *Make a Real Living as a Freelance Writer* (Nomad Press, 2004)

An absolute necessity for the mom (or dad) who wants to pursue the writing life. Christina Katz' brutal honesty and excellent examples take a scary concept (getting published) and make it approachable. Even though the book's focus is the mom in the household, the advice easily applies to the writing dad as well.

Jeff Ayers, *Voyages of Imagination: The Star Trek Fiction Companion* (Star Trek, 2006)

Thinking about juggling a writing career with raising children? You must read *Writer Mama* first, where you'll get the inside scoop on everything from landing those first clips to interviewing when you have a toddler underfoot. Christina Katz maps out the journey between the playground and the Major Leagues of freelancing with wit, style, and a can-do attitude.

Diana Burrell, *The Renegade Writer's Query Letters That Rock* (Marion Street Press, 2006)

From the beginning writer to the experienced freelancer, *Writer Mama* helps you navigate the steps to getting published, winning assignments, and earning money—all without leaving the comfort of your home. Using examples from successful writer mamas and concrete tips on how to submit to editors, *Writer Mama* introduces you to important terminology, proper editor etiquette, and simple ways to break into freelancing.

Wendy Burt, *Oh, Solo Mia!* (McGraw-Hill, 2001) and *Work It, Girl!* (McGraw-Hill, 2003)

Like taking a writing class at your neighborhood playground—*Writer Mama* is a must-have resource that speaks to the specific challenges of the writing parent with advice from those with one eye on the monkey bars and another on their manuscript.

Sharon Miller Cindrich, journalist, columnist, and author of *E-Parenting: Keeping Up With Your Tech-Savvy Kids* (Random House, 2007)

Christina Katz takes a stay-at-home-mom and turns her into a dragon-slayer with all the tools to make a writing career not just feasible, but downright practical. My copy of this book is wrought with notes, dog-eared pages, and highlighted resources, earning it a place on my reference shelf.

C. Hope Clark, author of *The Shy Writer* (Book Locker, 2004) convinced, here are ten reasons why you can launch a writing career alongside your kids that can take you from anonymous wannabe to established author:

1. **More mamas are publishing, as mamas, for mamas, and more.** Motherhood is in. More editor and agent moms are considering careers as writers. What's more, writer mamas, editor mamas, and agent mamas are suddenly becoming more visible. If you are a writer mama, rejoice! As a reader or subscriber, you may have already heard about publications such as *Literary Mama* (online zine for writing moms), *Hip Mama* (zine with print and online versions), and *Brain, Child* (print magazine). And more publications by moms, for moms are popping up every day. Zines, whether appearing in print, e-mail (e-zine) or online (online zine) are becoming increasingly popular. It's nice to be hip for a change!

2. **More moms are working from home, both full and part time.** You are not alone. More moms are already working from home, thanks to technological advances that make this more convenient and affordable than ever. Trend expert Faith Popcorn predicted this phenomenon back in the 1980s in her book *The Popcorn Report*. Call us WAHMs (work-at-home-moms), call us mompreneurs, call us what you will: More SAHMs (stay-at-home-moms) are determined to make working from home an option. And writers are no exception. A study by the American Society of Journalists and Authors (ASJA) concluded that the typical professional freelance journalist is female (73 percent), married (65 percent), and has at least one child (58 percent).

3. **Pssst: Writer mamas support and encourage each other.** The supposed "Mommy Wars" are bunk among writers. If you don't believe me, check out one of the many Web sites devoted to providing support for writing moms: www. momwriters.com, www.writefromhome.com, and www.thewritermama.com,

to name a few. There's a whole lot of supporting going on. (Just be sure you don't get so busy socializing with everyone *about* writing that you don't get your actual writing done.)

4. You can learn to write in your own backyard (or online). If you have one eye on the bank account and the other on landing assignments, it makes sense to start with classes that will help you raise your income, rather than those that will run up a huge student loan. Community college classes are reasonably priced. Online classes are reasonably priced. And regional writers' conferences are just a short drive away. There is no question that classes and workshops are the best places to learn about the needs and wants of the publishing industry, where you can find your niche, and how to streamline your efforts and get published.

5. Mamas who write set a good example for their kids. Motherhood is no excuse *not* to write; it's a great reason to start! Our children deserve happy parents who find their vocation and pursue it. If your days at home with your kids are numbered, taking tiny steps toward your writing and publishing goals can start rewriting "the writing on the wall." Start today, and you'll be one step closer.

6. Writing gets done in small increments (and that's the only time mamas have). Happy is the mom who has accepted her life circumstances and is working to be just a tiny bit more productive every day. That's a writer mama who is going to persevere. Staying sane requires doing what you can do, not simply wishing to do more than you already do. Wishing and taking action: Not the same thing. Become a mom who takes action toward her goals today. (And if you're reading this book, you already are!)

7. **Writing careers grow right alongside your kids.** Writing is a journey, not an event. There is a sane path to combining writing and motherhood, and it involves creating an environment in which you can focus on getting one task done at a time. One day you will be amazed at how prolific you have become, writing a little bit here and a little bit there, while improving your writing skills (a.k.a. your "craft") the more you practice. Then publishing will no longer be the dream, but the norm. And then you'll need a new challenge, right? We'll talk about that in the final section of this book.

8. **Many mamas "make it" eventually.** In the old days, I wondered if I would ever "make it" as a writer. Today, I know that success or failure was in my hands all along. As the diminutive designer Edna Mode says in the animated movie *The Incredibles*, "Luck favors the prepared, dahling." I can now tell the difference between the ways I procrastinate compared to constructive writing and marketing habits I've developed and repeat because they work for me. The former brought me no closer to getting my name into print; the latter gets me into print more often. These days, you cannot pick up a daily newspaper without reading a mom writer's success story. That's good news for all of us.

9. **More opportunities are available to connect with professional writer mamas.** The Web offers access to professional writers like never before. Because of growing pressure to have a Web presence, most working-mom writers are available via their Web site, blog, or e-mail. Start connecting with published writers by dropping a note to express your appreciation for her work; or, if you already have a little experience, offer to do an interview or profile for the learning experience. Maybe you'll make an article sale while you're at it. Keeping in casual touch with published mom writers will help you become one.

10. **The creative mama renaissance is here!** Moms' voices are diverse, significant, and worthy. And moms are strong in numbers—about eighty million in the U.S. alone. But there is no "club" of writer mamas entitled to speak for all moms, leaving your voice out in the cold. There are simply those writer mamas who have gone ahead and set a good example—who have clarified what they want to say, cultivated their writing skills, and practiced communicating effectively—and you can too. So don't allow others to speak for you. Allow them to inspire you to express yourself clearly and with authority because that's when readers start to listen.

Time to Work for It

Beginning writers need to remember that it isn't talent alone that sets you apart from the crowd. Just as important are appropriateness of your ideas, attention to detail, professionalism, and follow-through. Believe me, there are plenty of writers out there who write well. But there is a shortage of writers who take their writing seriously without taking themselves too seriously. Practice thinking of yourself as a professional, even if you are novice or a hobbyist. Get out of your own way and become willing to learn from people who are clearly qualified to offer you sound advice. Apply what you learn immediately and pay attention to how considering and applying suggestions affects your publication success rate in the short and long run. Then, and only then, can you take your writing and your marketing skills to the next natural level in your career—through experience, not speculation.

In the past, a mom who wanted to write may not have been able to find even an ounce of encouragement anywhere. You'll find not only encouragement in this book, but also insight into how to think like a working writer. You also receive fair warning that the leaps from one task to the next will be challenging. This book is divided into four sections to echo the progression of a typical career. There is no predicting how long it will take, but if you were to look back later on the twists and turns of your career path, you'd see something like this in the rearview:

Preparation (covering chapters one to six) will help you adopt the tools and attitudes successful writer mamas use to match their ideas to their next, best byline.

Practice (chapters seven to twelve) shows step-by-step how to build basic writing skills you'll need to compete with pros who have been writing for years. You'll practice basic forms of writing, from tips all the way to full-length articles and essays, and learn how and when to submit them with a basic cover letter.

Professionalism (chapters thirteen to eighteen) will take your newfound skills and confidence and apply them to the task of querying for assignments. You'll learn when you really need to query instead of sending a cover letter and learn how to complete longer assignments without losing your balance.

Poise (chapters nineteen to twenty-three) helps you develop crucial skills for "producing" yourself and your writing career, so you can become known well-enough to garner the attention of agents and editors and move on to pitching and writing nonfiction books.

So forget all about formulas guaranteed to make you an overnight best-seller—writing is a rhythm, not a formula. This book will help you find your rhythm by putting you through the paces of preparation, practice, professionalism, and poise. The rest happens naturally because writing careers are just as organic as anything meaningful and lasting. So why not raise yours the same way you raise your kids? Day after day after day. And why not begin today?

I.
Preparation

1

Accumulate Ideas

> About thirty seconds after I got my positive pregnancy test, a hundred questions ran through my mind, every one of them a potential article. One of the greatest things about being a writer is that I can get paid for getting answers to my own questions! Boy, when my morning sickness lets up, I'll be unstoppable.
>
> ~ JENNA GLATZER, EXPECTING

From the time you wake up in the morning until the time you go to sleep at night (even if you don't necessarily get to sleep at night), you have an advantage over the rest of the work-a-day world—the thoughtful moments that are built into an average mom's day. I bet you spend some time each day rocking the baby, strolling the baby, and driving the baby around town in his or her car seat. Even if your preferred mode of transportation is bicycle, moms generally have built-in reflection time that isn't always available to others.

This is good news because writing for publication begins with ideas, and one of your primary assets as a writer is going to be your ability to come up with appropriate ideas to suit specific editorial needs.

Joining the Conversation

Think of writing for publication like entering a conversation being carried on by folks who don't necessarily know you—if you were joining a chat amongst perfect strangers, you probably wouldn't just rudely interrupt and shout, "Hey, I've got a great idea for you!" Right?

Furthermore, if you were going to participate in a public dialogue (which is basically what it means to publish your words), you would take some time to pull your thoughts together, consider how you would be perceived by your audience, and do everything possible to communicate effectively, right? The same is true of joining the conversations taking place among publications and their readerships. It's not about you or how brilliantly you write or how amazing your ideas are. Without appropriateness, your ideas will fall on deaf ears. Think instead about ways you can enliven the publication's conversation and draw more people into it.

Writing Is a Response

Ideas generally happen in response to something already written or to an event from everyday life or both (and sometimes seemingly out of nowhere). This is why responding to the happenings in your everyday life is often the best place for beginning writers to start. So before you consider the appropriate audience, publication, and guidelines for presenting your ideas to editors (all topics that we will cover later), it helps to get in the habit of responding to what's going on in your own life. Don't be afraid to write in order to hear yourself think—jot a quick response to your ideas right when they come to you. It will help you synthesize them. Sometimes responses crop up while journaling or drafting; blogs are a popular place for writers to give opinions on diverse topics, often based on something heard or read. (See the sidebars in this chapter on journaling and blogging.) If you can make responsiveness a habit, you can capture details that pay off later when you write on a topic for a specific publication.

I'd be willing to bet, as a mom, you are no stranger to responsiveness. So let's talk about your day. I bet you could come up with a hundred ideas from one day if you were

🐝 Journal for Ideas (and Sanity!)

With mouths to feed, bodies to wash, laundry to fold, and hubbies to meet halfway, it's easy for moms to lose touch with personal priorities. One way to reconnect with yourself is to set aside at least a half hour daily for writing in your journal. Your goal is not to write anything of interest to anyone else, nor even, necessarily, to yourself. What you're really after is a dumping ground for the garbage that has gotten into your head and needs a way out.

Your journal doesn't have to be fancy or fine. A legal pad, a spiral-bound notebook or—if you like to doodle or use markers—a sketchpad all work well. Choose a format in which you feel comfortable letting it all hang out. It will help you reclaim a little corner of your day and your mind so you can declare it yours, all yours.

asked (or asked yourself) some questions. So let's ask a few here (look for more in the chapter exercise):

- What did you notice about your day today?
- What might someone else find interesting about your day?
- Which parts of your experience do you wish to write about?

Published writing often begins with ideas that arrive quietly. If you are not paying attention, you won't notice them and they will slip right by. Sometimes beginning writers think, "Oh, someone has already written about my idea." But instead of dismissing your idea, cultivate your response to what has been written on the topic and then see where you can go with your idea from there.

Mama, Meet the Zeitgeist

When you're a mom, the prospect of keeping up with the latest trends can feel daunting. Most of us are just trying to keep up with everybody's ever-changing schedules! But if you can tap into the Zeitgeist ("the spirit of the time"), you can tap into what's on everybody's mind, and editors will feel the resonance and value for their readership. Here's how to tap into the trends without a major time investment.

Rhymes with "chutney." Pick up a copy of *Utne Reader* magazine (formerly called *Utne*). Second in Zeitgeist-value only to trend guru Faith Popcorn's predictions, the value of this slim monthly volume is awesome. In my early days as a freelancer, I would simply read the latest issue and then riff off an article on one or a combination of the topics and voilà: an article I could resell over and over, year after year, because the ideas in *Utne Reader*'s pages are still dawning on the masses. Another publication that is interesting and forward-thinking, if you want to go global, is

Britain's *Ode* magazine. If you already write, you can use the topic ideas in these publications to freshen up some of your old topics.

Newspapers. Rip that daily (or weekly or regional) newspaper to shreds. Go ahead, get 'geisty (and inky too!)—tear out every article you think is interesting for whatever reason and tuck it in a tickler file or box. And consider this: The headliner in a newspaper will most likely show up next in magazines. So don't be afraid to scoop fresh ideas from small publications and take them to wider audiences.

Cruise the bookstore. In the early days of my freelancing career, I had an aversion to newspapers. So instead of picking up the day's news, I'd head to the bookstore and cruise the aisles, taking note of what was popular on the shelves, magazine

 Start a Blog

Blogs are a popular place for writers to respond to diverse topics, often based on something they hear or read. When you start your own blog, you create a public forum for your thoughts, ideas, and responses for a particular audience. In effect, you initiate a new conversation in a long line of conversations already initiated by other moms in other blogs. But the world can never have too many moms expressing themselves. I recommend you start a blog as a practice space for turning your private thoughts into a public discussion because that's what published writers do.

However, don't think that writing for publication and blogging are exactly the same thing, because they're not. And you may find, as you do the exercises and apply what you learn, that you have less and less time for your blog and become busier and busier writing for publication! There are other good reasons to keep blogging, even as you work on getting published, and we will discuss those in section four. Don't worry about "doing it right." Just pick a topic that matters to you and an audience you feel comfortable addressing and let it rip.

covers, and bestseller lists. Think of it as around-the-Zeitgeist in thirty minutes. This is a great activity for a weekend day, with a hot beverage in hand, when Dad or Grandma is watching the kids. You can also zoom in on the book sections that speak to your best audiences and glean loads of great ideas.

Turn on the tube. Be like Sherlock Holmes, only with a remote control instead of a magnifying glass. I know, this is usually a guy's job—but pick up that remote control and surf the airwaves. See what's going on. Get the name of the show, the type of show, and the gist of the show. Then move on. If you have the weekly TV guide, that can help, especially if you have—heaven forbid, for your writing's sake—satellite. (However, if you do, TiVo might come in handy. You can use it to search and record all the shows you find intriguing. How cool is that?)

Mirror, mirror. When I look in the mirror, I see a forty-year-old mama more concerned about what she thinks than what she looks like. (I figure I can always get a makeover.) Now it's your turn: top to bottom. See that mom in the mirror there? She is you. What do you notice about this woman that others might identify with? Is she going gray on top? Getting wrinkles around her mouth? Starting to sag in all those sag-prone places? Or perhaps she looks pretty darn good for woman her age. If not, don't despair—this is research. It's all grist for the writing mill.

The personal *is* political. When your child comes home with a black eye thanks to a bully at school, you are getting a glimpse of the Zeitgeist. When my daughter went to the hospital for five thousand dollars' worth of dental work caused by nighttime breastfeeding, it was an abrupt wake-up call from the Zeitgeist. The Geist is also calling you when you get an invitation in the mail to a local artist's show, an e-mail solicitation to be more politically involved, or a phone request to volunteer to lead the local Girl Scout meeting. That's the Zeitgeist knocking on your door, right in your own backyard.

Nesting is great. But even busy as you are, if you want to write for publication, you need to keep up with the big picture. Stay tuned in to the spirit of the times and you'll infuse your words with relevance and salability.

Front-Load Your Idea Bank

Using a convenient collection system, fill your idea bank with ideas sparked by these prompts. Make a list of:

- every place you have ever lived
- all the jobs you have ever had
- the seasons or holidays you love
- all the words that describe you
- everything you are good at, or simply know how to do
- topics on which you are already an expert, whether others know it or not
- all your current or past hobbies
- topics that have been on your mind lately, especially those you've already been writing about in your journal or blog
- the one topic you would choose if you had to write about only one topic for a whole year

As Nora Ephron says, "Everything in your life is material." It's your material. Use it! If how to use these ideas isn't immediately apparent, contain them. You are just getting warmed up.

Idea-Keeping

Ideas are ephemeral. They flit through your consciousness while you are taking the baby for a jog, chauffeuring the gang to soccer practice, or standing in the middle of the grocery store. Before you can capture them on paper, Woosh! They're gone as quickly as they came. That's okay because I've got several suggestions of ways to track your ideas once you have them.

When your ideas are in order, your mind can relax, like in a well-kept home. But where will you keep all these ideas? How will you keep track of them? Trust me, if you don't, you will be sorry when you see someone else has written on and published *your* ideas (even more sorry if they did a good job; *double* sorry if they did a poor job). If you don't already have an effective system for containing your ideas, think about which of these might work for you. Here's how a few professional mom writers capture their ideas.

Real Simple Mama: Even the most harried mama can use author Elizabeth Rusch's system—the basic yellow legal pad. On one page she keeps her list of things to do and on the back side she lists her ideas—all of them. This is how she realized, after writing for an adult audience for many years, that she wanted to switch and give some of her children's book ideas a chance. Today she has eight children's book manuscripts in various phases of development. In the past year, two have found publishers.

Freelance journalist Kelly James-Enger takes the notebook (or legal-pad) system a step further. She uses a notebook to compile her ideas by hand and then transfers them a couple times a month into a computer document. One benefit of this method is the ease of arranging ideas by genre or audience—just copy and paste under the appropriate category.

Process-Oriented Mama: For me, ideas often come from the process of writing. For a decade, part of my daily routine has been to write three pages of longhand, stream-of-consciousness gibberish (aka journaling). Naturally, ideas pop up along the way. Some are subdued, while others seem to bounce up and down on the page. Ideas that I'm excited about get written in big, bold letters at the top of the page or in the left-hand margin. If the idea is ready to pop right then and there, I go to the computer and start typing. If you have a blog, your ideas may emerge there in a similar way. Make them officially part of your idea collection.

On-the-Go Mama: Ideas often come, as diarist Anaïs Nin said, not while we are at our desks writing, but while we are in the midst of living. But the problem with too many notepads (in your kitchen, in your car, in your purse) is that ideas must then be collected and transferred to the Mama-of-All-Ideas List. Try using author Anne Lamott's method: Don't leave home without a note card and pen crammed in your back pocket. Ideas written on note cards can be organized in a card file, tossed in a desk drawer, or tacked up on a bulletin board when you get home.

Visual Mama: Diana Burrell, an author and freelancer for national magazines like *Parenting* and *SELF,* has a trick she uses to remember her ideas while she's out and about with her son, whom she calls her "little money-maker."

> If I'm running errands, I've trained my brain to remember story ideas until I get home. For example, if I think about writing a story about mini-bananas and another on avoiding food coloring in foods, I think about #1 being the 'big banana' and imagine a giant banana for a few seconds. I think about #2 with a label that reads 'Blue #2.' When I get home I just imagine #1 and #2 and remember the banana and the food-coloring label in my mind. That's enough to trigger my brain into remembering the ideas.

Bigger-Is-Better Mama: Sometimes Post-Its and notepads are too small for writers with big ideas. In this case, try using poster paper taped to the wall or stick scraps of paper on a large bulletin board. You might also arrange Post-Its on a white board in storyboard fashion, or to keep track of your to-write list. This process can also be used to create a visual tickler file of images, articles, and photographs that illustrate your idea. Think of it as brainstorming space either for juggling multiple projects or sketching out a challenging sequence. That's what I do.

Final word: If there is one habit that will get your career off to an energetic start, it's getting your thoughts down on the page and keeping them around until you're ready to use them. So err in the direction of having too many ideas, and regularly revisit and update your list to generate more great ideas on the spot.

Determine the idea-keeping system or systems that make you more prolific. One approach is to try several systems at once and abandon those that aren't working. Another is to let the way you track ideas evolve over time (like everything else). Just remember the key: Immediate access to your ideas when you need them.

2

Identify Your Audiences

> To me, there is no such thing as a good idea or a bad idea. There's an idea that you can sell to a particular magazine, and there's an idea that is a perfectly good idea that will not sell to a magazine, at least not a magazine you want to write for.
>
> ~ ELIZABETH RUSCH, MOTHER OF TWO

Your readers will be everybody, right? Nope.

The most successful writers are intimately acquainted with their audiences and know the best way to speak to them, but you can't be that tuned into everybody. You have to narrow your focus.

Most moms start writing for an audience just like themselves. And yet, because it seems so obvious, audience identification can be tricky if you over-sympathize with your audience or if don't think about them enough. Spend time understanding your most natural audiences, because this step may well make the difference between writing for a specific readership and writing for no one at all.

Take a Closer Look at What You Read

All published materials, from bestsellers to blogs, have a clearly defined target audience. If you subscribe to or read a magazine regularly, chances are good that you fall into its target market.

Take a complete inventory of what you read. Empty your magazine rack, check your coffee table, look on your bookshelves and your nightstand for every book, magazine, newspaper, and newsletter. And don't stop there. Open the Favorites folder in your Internet browser and see what you can see. Are you beginning to notice a pattern in your reading habits? List all of your top reads by name, type of publication, and name of the publishing company, like these samples:

> **Books:** *Operating Instructions: A Journal of My Son's First Year*, by Anne Lamott. Anchor.

> **Magazines/Periodicals:** *Better Homes and Gardens*; *Bargain Style*. Meredith Publishing Group.

> **Newspapers:** *The Oregonian*. Metro newspaper. Newhouse News.

Online Publications: BlueSuitMom.com. Advice for professional mothers. BSM Media.

Examine Your Roles

To choose a good first audience, look at those you easily identify with and branch out from there. Start by jotting down keywords that describe you. Yes, it's labeling or stereotyping, but stay with it. For example, here are some of mine. I am a:

Woman

Wife

Mother

Parent

Writer

Teacher

Friend

Daughter

Sister

Easy enough, so far? Now choose at least nine words that describe you. They won't all be the same as mine, but keep them fairly straightforward for now.

First Audiences for Moms

Circle a few potential audiences that might fit with you:

- Brides
- Business People
- Fitness Buffs
- Dieters
- Health Enthusiasts
- Financial Whizzes and/or Flops
- Parents
- Newlyweds
- Moms or Women
- Foodies
- Athletes
- Gardeners
- Techies
- Home decorators
- Travelers
- Arts Aficionados

From these nine, narrow your list down to your top four. They may be the words that strike you as particularly pertinent to you today. They may be related to ideas that have been on your mind recently. Or they may be your top four of all time. Use your instincts and don't overthink it. This is not the time to choose "daughter" because your mother would be disappointed if you didn't. This is the time to say, "I'm picking lover because I've been thinking about sex a lot lately."

Your keywords will now be put to work finding your best audiences. On a blank page, draw a pie chart (Cathy Belben gave me the idea for this step of the process): first a good-sized circle; then two lines, from top to bottom and side to side, to divide your pie into quarters. Just beyond the outer edge of each quarter-slice of pie, write one of your top four keywords.

Then, use a table to explore your keywords in a little more detail before you fill in each quarter-slice of pie. Start by listing your keywords in the left-hand column, then ask, "What characterizes me in this role?" Some of my expanded topics look like this:

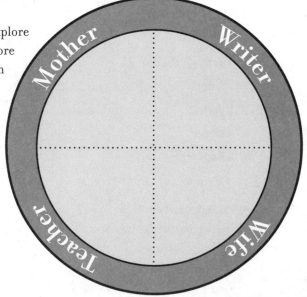

Audience	Description	Description	Description
Mother	Advanced maternal age—"AMA"	Attachment parenting	Co-parenting
Writer	Moms and writing	Becoming an author	How to land a book deal
Wife	Gaining weight after childbirth	Married younger man	Interfaith weddings
Teacher	Writing and publishing	Authentic career	Right-brain approach

Write down what sets you apart from, or connects you to, the norm. Write whatever pops into your head and don't be too picky. The point is to dig deeper into potential material for each of your chosen audiences. Once you have some ideas to work with, ask, "Who specifically would identify with or be interested in these topics?" Brainstorm specific descriptions until your audiences distinguish themselves from the crowd, like "Generation X moms," "Holistic moms," "Creative moms," or "Literary-minded moms." I can think of four magazines right off the top of my head that these types of moms might read (and you will be able to as well, once you familiarize yourself with a variety of publications):

> **Generation X Moms:** *Hip Mama* (zine)
>
> **Holistic Moms:** *Mothering*

If you want to learn how to write well enough for national publication someday, you might actually be better off studying articles written not for your chosen audience, but for one you wouldn't typically read. Why? Because articles in your best-audience publications are difficult to study when you are distracted by all of the tips, ads, product recommendations, and photos targeting someone just like you.

For example, if you aspire to write for an audience of affluent, urban women, grab a couple of magazines that target affluent, urban men. (Look for a sexy woman on the cover and ads inside for luxury cars, men's jewelry, and expensive alcohol.) Take a good, hard look at the articles you find in there, both long and short. What can you learn about magazine publishing, in general, and how to write for a targeted audience, specifically, by studying a totally different type of magazine than you usually read? A whole lot.

Creative Moms: Mary Engelbreit's *Home Companion*

Literary-minded Moms: *Brain, Child*

Transfer the name of the publication into the pie-chart section where it fits. Then go back to your original list of publications you already read. Do any of them fit into your slices of pie (audiences)? If so, fill them in. As a reader, already familiar with their tone, content, and style, you are uniquely qualified to write for them.

As you move along the regular grooves of everyday life, you'll start noticing new publications that fit your top four audiences, publications you never noticed before. Could they become publications you could potentially write for? Heck yeah. Start collecting (see the sidebar "Finding Your Audience at the Magazine Rack" later in this chapter for more information about this process). It will be a lot easier now that you can run the thousands of magazines out there through the filter of your best-bet audiences. When you're starting out, this can diminish the feeling of being overwhelmed or going off in too many directions at the same time.

Now that you are getting in the habit of audience identification, you will be able to do it on the fly for any publication that comes at you. Of course, you won't choose publications to suit only your best audiences forever because that would limit your success in the long run. When you're ready to branch out, you'll know how. Simply add another audience to your list. But start out by identifying the audiences that suit you best and collecting as many publications for those specific audiences as possible, and you'll be prepared to make the most of each of your ideas.

The Benefits of Freelancing

Freelancing teaches you valuable lessons about your business strengths and weaknesses while helping you establish published credits. By practicing some basic journalism skills, you can work your way up the writing ranks and increase your chances of literary success in the short and long run. By freelancing, you will learn about and get used to:

- Partnering with editors and being edited
- Taking assignments and meeting deadlines
- Finding your unique style and voice
- Strengthening your writing craft
- Being self-employed
- Taking pride in doing your best work

If that doesn't convince you, here are a couple more benefits:

Freelancing reduces mommy mush-mind. One of the most distressing things about being the mother of young children is that your brain often feels like it has turned to mush. Moms spend so much time goo-goo-ga-ga-ing that, when reintroduced to the company of adults, it's easy to feel like a kid at the grownups' table. Writing with specific short-term goals in mind is a mental challenge and an outlet for creativity, inspirations, and ideas, which feels especially good when what you hear all day begins with "Hey mommy! Hey mama! Hey mom!" So give your mind an adult-level workout and see how you feel afterward. The opportunity to focus on a goal will help your mind feel sharper, and soon you'll be back among the articulate!

Freelancing is a mental stress-buster. Writing short articles can help you break up the arduous yet monotonous tasks that comprise day-to-day life as a mother. Mixing up writing breaks with daily chores can help you focus, take your mind off problems, and even help you work through some of those crises that are bound to crop up when you're the only adult home all day.

And remember, every writer has to start somewhere. This isn't the end of the road, it's just the beginning! Julia Cameron started out as a journalist. Anne Lamott wrote restaurant reviews. Barbara Kingsolver credits journalism with forcing her away from her computer to meet people she would not otherwise see.

Start simple, diversify later. Novelist Jennie Shortridge, author of *Eating Heaven* and *Riding With the Queen*, didn't start out as a novelist; she simply knew that was where she wanted to end up.

> I left a corporate marketing job in 1995 and started freelancing for local and re-gional magazines, then national ones. My dream was always to write and publish fiction, and writing shorter nonfiction pieces actually helped me learn to write in a concise way, on a deadline, and to do it every day. I also learned a little about how the publishing world works and began to make important connections that have served me well throughout my writing career. For instance, my editors at *Glamour* and *Mademoiselle* are both now authors themselves, and provided blurbs for my novels.

Start short, come back to short later. Plenty of writers, having scaled the moun-tain called Writing a Book, continue to write articles because it provides welcome mental relief (not to mention money) from longer, more arduous projects. Author and freelancer Wendy Burt has published more than five hundred articles, and despite her author status, she still returns to the short stuff to keep herself happily productive.

> On any given day I will be working on three or four projects—usually in different genres. If I've got a boring business article to edit, I'll take a break to work on some fun greeting cards or bumper sticker ideas. I'll go back to editing the business article then "reward" myself by working on a short story or filler.

Flexibility is good. Show me a group of mom writers at the peak of their careers and I will show you writers who didn't and don't balk when it comes to writing nonfiction along with, and often alongside, everything else.

3

Tear Apart Target Markets

> I pitched several ideas to the editor of *Wondertime*, one of which was accepted. The work—writing, interviewing, rewriting, wordsmithing—was more rigorous than I'd anticipated, but in May 2006, I got to read my article in a national glossy (and, yes, there is something special about holding a magazine with your name in it).
>
> ~ JOANNA NESBIT, MOTHER OF TWO

According to the industry association Magazine Publishers of America, there were 18,267 magazines published in North America in 2005. A 2005 report by the Newspaper Association of America counted over two thousand newspapers in circulation in the U.S. and Canada. When you factor in the new online publications emerging daily, it's no wonder beginning writers feel overwhelmed about how to get published and where to submit.

There is only one way to take the next step in your writing and publishing journey: Zoom in on one of your first four target audiences and learn to analyze markets like a pro. You chose four audiences in chapter two as the most appropriate market categories for you to approach initially. Pull that list back out. We're going to take it with us to visit *Writer's Market*, a guide to the publishing industry.

I chose Mothers, Writers, Wives, and Teachers. If you also chose Mothers, your closest market category in *Writer's Market* is "Child Care & Parental Guidance," under Consumer Magazines. If you chose Writers, your closest market category is "Journalism & Writing," under Trade Magazines.

Market Research 101

Do Some Quick Research on Four Magazines in the Same Category

Quickly compare and contrast four magazines within one market category (Child Care & Parental Guidance or one of the others) to see how they differ in content, style, and tone. This can be done with four magazines in about twenty minutes using an Internet browser with a high-speed connection and search engine. You can use the links provided in the online version of *Writer's Market* to find a magazine's home page, or type keywords into a search engine to get to the specific page you need. Try searching by: "[Name-of-magazine] magazine, advertising, or media kit." Once you practice this a few times, you'll have

- **B.O.B.** "Back of the book." The final section of the magazine where you can often find shorter pieces and essays and sometimes even tips.
- **Byline.** Your name as it will appear with your article (usually at the beginning but sometimes at the end (e.g., by Christina Katz).
- **Contributor or Contributing Editor.** Freelancers, or experts in their field, who publish frequently in the magazine, usually on an extended contract basis.
- **Departments.** Sections devoted to a topic (e.g., health, beauty, or time for you).
- **Evergreen.** Type of article that is published over and over, seasonally or otherwise consistently (e.g., parental discipline strategies or how to spring clean your home).
- **F.O.B.** "Front of the book." The first section of the magazine where you can often find shorter pieces and the departments.
- **Market Guide.** A book or online database listing markets interested in working with freelancers.
- **Masthead.** A listing of the editorial, artistic, and design staff, typically found in the first few pages of a magazine or newspaper. Often includes a list of contributors or contributing editors. Sometimes the sales staff is listed on the same page, sometimes on a separate page.
- **Media Kit.** Marketing statistics and advertising information sent out to potential advertisers of a publication. Often includes an editorial calendar.
- **Well or Feature Well.** The middle of the magazine where the feature-length articles appear.

it down to twenty minutes, no problem. But don't get sidetracked, or it will take much longer. If you have access to the print edition of the magazines, check those out, too. Often the two are very different. The print edition may help you learn more about article format and length.

Parents Magazine	*Parenting* Magazine
Circulation: 2.2 million	**Circulation:** 2.15 million
Publisher: Gruner + Jahr, NY	**Publisher:** Time, Inc., NY
Frequency: 12/year	**Frequency:** 12/year
Slogan: *We're everywhere*	**Slogan:** *What really matters to moms*
Content: "American family," "For parents," raise happy, healthy children	**Content:** "For moms," emotional support, mom-tested info, really useful ideas
Voice: Practical	**Voice:** Mother-to-mother
Ed. Calendar: No	**Ed. Calendar:** No
Media Kit: No	**Media Kit:** Yes
Online content: Yes	**Online content:** Yes
Child Magazine	*Mothering* Magazine
Circulation: 1 million	**Circulation:** 100,000
Publisher: Meredith, NY	**Publisher:** Independent, Santa Fe, NM
Frequency: 10/year	**Frequency:** Bimonthly
Slogan: *Raising kids with smarts and style*	**Slogan:** *Natural family living*
Content: Timely info, experts, trends, breakthroughs, alternative/traditional mix	**Content:** Holistic, nurturing, inspirational, politics of childbirth, researched, from-the-heart
Voice: Upscale	**Voice:** Down-to-earth
Ed. Calendar: Yes	**Ed. Calendar:** Yes
Media Kit: Yes	**Media Kit:** Yes
Online content: Yes	**Online content:** Yes

Work With One Target Market at a Time

Based on the contrasting information you gathered in your table and a quick read of each magazine, you should be able to decide which magazine is the most natural fit for you. As a bonus, you'll already have a good idea how it differs from its competitors. If you feel a strong connection to more than one publication, pick one for now and dig deeper into other choices later.

Identify Every Freelance Opportunity You Can Find

If you are a beginning freelancer, you may not realize just how many publishing opportunities exist within one magazine issue. Using the May 2006 issue of *Parenting* as an example, what can you learn by analyzing one publication extensively and taking notes? If you can get your hands on a copy, follow along while you look over the shoulder of an experienced freelancer:

Study the cover. The cover tells you, at a glance, what matters to the magazine. Cover photo (mother and child—focus on the child). Cover title topics (trying new foods, baby learning people skills, change how you discipline, raising a can-do kid, handling child emergencies, nine toys that teach).

What Freelancers Never Write

Take a quick peek at what freelancers don't write. When you see the "negative space" more clearly, you'll better realize just how much editorial space there is to fill in a magazine (generally speaking, about 40–50 percent). Freelancers never write:

- Ad copy
- Advertorials (these ads are specifically designed to resemble editorial content, and are generally not generated by freelancers except in some special newspaper sections)
- Letters from the editor
- Anything that isn't an article, interview, profile, essay, filler, or review.

Examine the table of contents. The table of contents tells you how the editorial material is organized and categorized for readers. (*Parenting* has a stages index for child ages one through twelve.) Callouts (cover stories at a glance, "For You;" by-the-ages index, parenting.com). Sections (Child Development, Healthy Kids, Family Time, Food, Every Issue).

Use the masthead. The editorial masthead page lists the names and titles of everyone in the editorial department. Use a sticky note to mark this page. You will compare the names in the bylines (the author credits) to the names in the masthead to determine what areas of the magazine are being filled by freelancers. Below, all of the articles in one issue of *Parenting* have been broken down into two columns—articles not written by freelancers (on the left) and those written by freelancers (on the right):

Not Freelance	*Freelance*
F.O.B. (FRONT OF BOOK)	F.O.B. (FRONT OF BOOK)
Editor's column, reader tips, reader roundups, etc.	"Kid's health" (byline, short bio, title: "Emergency! A no-panic guide to saving your child's life")
No paid tips, expert health column, smart solutions to reader questions (all in-house)	
"Work + Family" (associate editor)	
"Time-savers" (assistant editor)	
"Reality check" (contributing editor)	

Not Freelance	Freelance
SECTION: "ALL YOURS" "Your style" (editorial assistant) "Playtime" (contributing editor)	**SECTION: "ALL YOURS"** "Your Time" (byline only, title: "The Friend Connection") "Your Beauty" (filler, byline only, title: "6 fresh ways to brighten your look") "Your Health" (filler, byline only, title: "Yoga on the move") "Your Relationships" (personal essay, byline, short bio, title: "My Husband, the Magician")
THE FEATURE WELL "The Social Lives of Babies" (contributing editor) "Fun Toys That Teach" (selected by articles editor) Reader poll "The Best for a New Baby" (associate editor)	**THE FEATURE WELL** "How to Get Your Child to Try New Foods (and Like 'Em!)" (byline, bio). Format: Seven tips with recipe "I Did it Myself" (byline, bio). Format: Feature with four subheads and one sidebar "The Best Ways to Discipline" (byline, bio). Format: Multiple-choice quiz "The Kid Gap" (byline, bio). Format: four subheads by number of years kids are apart

Not Freelance	Freelance
B.O.B. (BACK OF BOOK)	B.O.B. (BACK OF BOOK)
"Mom Squad" (in-house)	"Ages+ Stages" section:
"Becoming a Mom, Becoming a	Ages 0-1: 3 freelancers, bylines only
Grandma" (book excerpt)	Ages 1-2: 3 freelancers, bylines only
"Dad's-Eye View"	Ages 2-3: 3 freelancers, bylines only
"Air Rage" (book excerpt)	Ages 3-5: 3 freelancers, bylines only
"Last Word"	Ages 5-8: 1 freelancers, byline only
"Haiku for Moms" (book excerpt)	Ages 8-12: 2 freelancers, bylines only
	"Parenting picks" (5 freelancers,
	bylines only)
	"Healthy Bites" (2 freelancers,
	bylines only)
	"Easy Cooking" (byline only)

So if you thought there weren't opportunities to get published in national magazines, think again! Every article in the right-hand column proves otherwise.

Put Your Markets Under the Magnifying Glass

In chapter two, you chose your top four magazines in one of your market categories. You used *Writer's Market* to select them and conduct quick Internet research to narrow your choices down to the one best magazine to approach first. Now study that magazine, taking notes on which articles are by freelancers. Once you've figured out which ones are by freelancers, you'll be ready to approach this publication with an intelligent and informed perspective.

Six Benefits of Being a Write-at-Home Mom

Two out of three stay-at-home moms today are starting home-based businesses. And writing is one of the few careers you can start part time with little or no start-up cost. Because of this, you can try it first to see if you like it before making a full-time commitment. While launching a writing career as a mom is challenging, the perks can make it truly worthwhile in the long run. These benefits encouraged writing moms to choose "professional writer" as their vocation, and they may encourage you too. Being a freelance allows you to:

1. **Explore your interests.** Are you passionate about fitness? Kelly James-Enger has written hundreds of articles on the topic. Do relationships fascinate you? Diana Burrell dives into their mysteries in her nationally published articles. Like to go straight to the top? Elizabeth Rusch takes her childrearing challenges straight to Ph.D.s, authors, and doctors. She says, "I get paid to interview national experts about problems that I'm facing as a parent, or issues that my kids are struggling with."

2. **Be helpful, or give back.** Writer Sharon Cindrich discovered that birth control options had made major strides when she was through with baby-making mode. So, at her annual doctor's appointment, she did what any sensible mom writer would do: She checked out her options and shared the results in an article for the *Milwaukee Journal-Sentinel*, her local newspaper. If you enjoy being of service to others, you will never run out of opportunities to educate, inform, and inspire readers.

3. **Gain self-confidence.** Moms who write professionally have an aura of queenliness about them. The reason they don't put up with any foolishness from anybody? They don't have the time! Being self-employed has a way of making you less uncertain and more assertive over time, and this sense of personal authority leads to better decision-making skills. The moral: Writing for publication can help you forge a stronger sense of self-confidence and self-worth.

4. **Channel ambition.** The modern word "freelance" originated from "free lance," a phrase coined by Sir Walter Scott in his 1819 novel *Ivanhoe* describing European mercenary soldiers from the fourteenth to sixteenth century. Motherhood is hardly a mercenary endeavor; perhaps this explains why motherhood and freelancing may seem so overwhelming at first glance. But learning to focus on and hit a clearly defined target is a great way to keep both sides of your brain in balance. So practice a little "Ready, Aim, Fire!" once in a while. It will do wonders to rebuild a sense of accomplishment that can feel absent after childbirth.

5. **Enjoy increased flexibility.** Writing moms know how to take a good hard look at the calendar, negotiate for extra writing time, write at odd hours, and still make deadlines no matter what germs (or other kinds of curveballs) invade their hallowed homes. When you make your own hours, you also get to change them when necessary. And though most writing moms work regular hours, they also have a certain amount of flexibility that folks with day jobs would envy.

6. **Create a handcrafted career.** While many writing careers resemble each other on the surface, one of the most exciting benefits of writing is being able to drop projects you're not crazy about and pursue those that suit you. Of course, sometimes you just need to pay the bills, and beginners can't be as choosy as pros. But with time and effort, you can ultimately design an à la carte writing career based on your personal priorities.

4

Digest the Guidelines

> One woman was publishing on the Internet eight years ago and her writing was raw, her punctuation dreadful, and her need to put herself into every story exhausting for her readers. But during these years she wrote daily, and each day she must have learned something new, for I found some of her work recently and it was beautifully crafted, engaging, and germane to readers everywhere. Hard work, daily writing, daily reading, and dedication to the craft will breed success.
>
> ~ PAM WHITE, MOTHER OF ONE

W hat are the things that editors want in an article that you need to know? You'll find the answers in writer's guidelines, which are especially important for beginning writers to read and digest. Writer's guidelines are directions, usually one or two pages, for writers to follow when submitting their work to a particular publication. Almost every publication that works with freelance writers makes them available to clarify their specific needs and wants. So eliminate the guesswork. Here is a list of the important topics you'll find in writer's guidelines:

- Pay rate (sometimes including when they pay—upon publication of your article, upon acceptance of your idea, or otherwise)
- Which editor to contact and his or her title
- The physical address, e-mail address (if provided) and URL of the publication
- How long they take to respond (when to follow up)
- A description of the publication and audience
- Strategies for breaking in and current editorial needs
- How to submit your writing (as a full manuscript or query via snail mail or e-mail)

Think of writer's guidelines as a recipe for success. Just like a recipe can help an inexperienced cook make cookies—the kind everyone wants to eat—writer's guidelines will guide the writer safely through the unfamiliar process of submitting work, a relationship satisfying to both the writer and editor.

And studying writer's guidelines is a snap compared to analyzing a publication's content. Used in conjunction, one can save time on the other. Especially since there are things you can get from one that you can't get from the other. For example, the critical information you find will qualify or disqualify you as a potential freelancer, "We only accept submissions from freelancers in our region" or "We only accept submissions that include quotes from people who live in our region." Well, if you are not from that region or don't have a method for getting quotes from that region on your topic, it probably won't make sense to spend any more time on that publication. It's simply not for you.

What you can't get from writer's guidelines is a sense for how to emulate the style of the publication's editorial content. Many writers depend on studying the articles to inform and fashion their submissions (strategies for doing this were offered in chapter three). This explains why the most common phrase in writer's guidelines is, "Please study the magazine before submitting." It sounds obvious, right? But too many writers don't, yet expect serious consideration without ever picking up the magazine. There is nothing worse than receiving inappropriate submissions when you've gone out of your way to inform writers how to approach your publication.

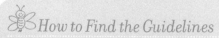 How to Find the Guidelines

Market guides you'll have to pay for (but it's worth it):

- *Writer's Market.* Book version updated annually; online version (www.Writers-Market.com) updated daily
- *The American Directory of Writer's Guidelines,* updated periodically
- Wooden Horse Publishing's "Magazines Database" (www.woodenhorsepub.com)
- Funds For Writers e-books (www.fundsforwriters.com) for fillers, essay markets, and online submissions

FREE market resources

- Writers Write "Writer's Guidelines Database" (www.writerswrite.com/writersguidelines/)
- Writing For DOLLARS Guidelines Database (www.writingfordollars.com/guidelines.cfm)
- Writer's Digest Top 100 "Hot Markets" (www.writersdigest.com)

Want to know the best reason to pay attention to what you find in writer's guidelines? As freelancer and author Sharon Cindrich always says, "To manage your expectations." Without guidelines you would be totally in the dark about who, what, when, where, why, and how to submit, because editors are too busy with the other responsibilities to disseminate this important information to every single writer who decides to send in a submission. So do yourself a favor: Don't just skim the writer's guidelines, study them before you submit. Before you know it, you'll be able to use them to help you tell the difference between a publication you can get published in and one you will never get published in.

Strategies for Success

Here's what you specifically need to pay attention to in writer's guidelines:

Any kind of editor-to-writer communication. Look for directions from the editor to writers, such as this one from *Family Circle* magazine: "Query letters should be concise and to the point. Also, writers should keep close tabs on *Family Circle* and other women's magazines to avoid

🍎 D.I.Y. Strategy for Finding Writer's Guidelines

Type one of the following into Google's search engine:

- "Writer's Guidelines [*Name of Magazine*]" (or whichever category you are seeking)
- "Submissions [*Name of Magazine*]"
- "[*Name of Magazine*] Editorial Calendar"

E-mail newsletters that include markets and/or market news:

- *Absolute Markets* (www.absolutewrite.com), free for the regular version, $15/year for the premium version
- *The Wooden Horse Publishing News Alert* (www.woodenhorsepub.com)
- *WritersWeekly* (www.writersweekly.com)
- *FundsforWriters* (www.fundsforwriters.com), free version or $12/year for the TOTAL version
- Worldwide Freelancer's weekly newsletter (www.worldwidefreelance.com)

submitting recently run subject matter." Aha. You just discovered that editors at *Family Circle* feel annoyed by writers who don't read enough back issues to know what ideas have recently been covered not just by *Family Circle* but by all women's magazines. Your mission then becomes *not* to be one of those writers.

Instructions for new writers on how to break in. You will usually find specific instructions for new writers in the guidelines. This is because editors know new writers need and want this information. So take them up on it. If an editor explicitly prefers to receive fillers or shorts from unfamiliar writers, then for goodness sakes, that's what you should send. This is how you let an editor know that you are not only conscientious, but also respectful and willing to work your way up the ranks.

Information that addresses your needs. There is no one size fits all when it comes to publications or their guidelines. Some writers are looking for publications that pay on acceptance vs. on publication. Others want to know how long they have to wait before they can resubmit an article elsewhere. Others still, especially when they are just getting started, will work extra hard to break into a publication they really admire or where they'd feel proud to be published. These are all legitimate things to look for in guidelines and are anticipated by the creators of guideline directories like the annual *Writer's Market* (comes in book or online form, links to guidelines when available online, more at www.writersmarket.com), Wooden Horse Database (online database only, magazines only at www.woodenhorsepub.com), and the most recent edition of *The American Directory of Writer's Guidelines* (a print-only compilation of writer's guidelines from magazine editors).

Make Sure the Editor Knows You Paid Attention

One way to make sure an editor knows that you are conscientious is to demonstrate it when you contact them, but in a casual way. For example, when you sit down to write your cover letter or query, make it clear that you read not only one, but several issues, of the magazine, just as the guidelines directed. You might do this by noting a detail or two from several different issues, in a way that is related to the topic of your correspondence. For example: "I noticed in your January 2006 cover story on Teen Battles that [the writer] discussed the pros and cons of *X* but did not mention *Y*" (insert what you noticed). This lets the editor know, in writing, that you were thorough in your preparation, and it begins to build a case for an article you can offer.

exercise

Go Get Those Guidelines!

Choose one of the publications that you have already studied. What more could you learn about the editor's wants and needs by obtaining and reading the guidelines? Can't find them? Go ahead and pick up the phone and call the editorial offices. Identify yourself as a freelancer looking for guidelines. Usually a secretary or assistant editor can point you in the right direction. Most likely they will give you the URL where they post their guidelines or send them to you via e-mail. Occasionally, you may need to send a good, old-fashioned SASE (self-addressed stamped envelope) to get them. Just include a brief request for writer's guidelines in business letter form (see chapter fifteen, pages 170–171) with your folded SASE in a business envelope and you'll receive your guidelines in a short time.

Scrounge for an Hour in the A.M.

Most writers, unless they are also parents, cannot possibly relate to the multiple challenges of kids and a career under one roof. No worries, though, because moms are experts at finding rhythms and routines that work best for everyone in the family. You can channel this wisdom into creating a schedule that gets your work done—even if you end up having to continually tweak it to keep up with your family's ever-changing needs.

Break your weekly tasks down in advance, based on what you think you can accomplish in the amount of time your kids will be occupied. Sunday night is a good time to do this. Make a simple weekly plan, even if you work at different times each day. A beginning writer might use such a plan to write one article per week while her kids watch *Sesame Street*.

If morning is your most mentally productive time of day, don't waste all your energy on things that could just as easily be done later in the day—like folding laundry, talking on the phone, checking e-mail, and making grocery lists.

What would simplify your morning routine? What gets your day off to a good start? What routines would help you set aside more early hours to write? Your answers to these questions will point you in the right direction. Here are some ideas for milking your mornings for every spare minute of writing time, regardless of your circumstances:

- Get up an hour earlier than usual. This may require going to bed an hour earlier at night. Perhaps you and your spouse could trade off night and morning duties: Your spouse oversees the bedtime routine and you oversee the morning routine—*after* you do your hour of early morning writing.

- Prepare lunches, set the table for breakfast, set up the coffee machine, and put out the non-perishable foods the night before. This simple ritual will better prepare you to meet your day, and it will give you precious extra time during the hectic morning hours.

- Create morning routines to suit each family member's personality so they will be self-directed and leave you to your writing. For example, your six year old may love to pick out his clothes the night before and lay them out on a chair for the next day, but your teenager may view this as a major violation of her rights. No need to micromanage; just work with each child to find the system that works for him or her. The operative word here is "works."

- Use television, VCRs, and DVDs in moderation, and as part of a regular routine that you can use for writing time. Kids like routines, and so do moms. Remind everyone involved that watching television is a special treat. Let the kids know you will be working while they watch, but are available if they need you. Explain that you expect them to behave and give them of preview of what's coming next. For example: "After *Barney*, we'll take a walk to the park (or have a play date, or go to soccer practice)."

- Don't forget morning activities that give you a little time here and there. Can you get a few notes written in the waiting room at a doctor appointment, or during children's classes or activities? Some groups require your participation, but others, especially after the toddler stage, don't. (In fact, they may prefer if you let them do their thing.) I recently roughed out several pages while Samantha was in a morning dance class, which came faster and more easily than anything I wrote in my office that day.

5

Tackle the Clips Catch-22

> *As a work-at-home mom, my world can sometimes feel a little narrow. Now that I have a monthly gig writing for a local arts magazine, I'm going out on assignments and meeting interesting people. By promoting local events, I feel like I'm making a contribution to my community. With each article I write, my world opens a little wider.*
>
> ~ LAUREN FRITZEN, MOTHER OF ONE

C lips are previously published samples of your writing. You can improve your chances of getting published at new publications by including clips with your submissions that show how well you have written for other publications. Of course, this leaves unpublished writers at a distinct disadvantage, which is why the topic of clips is often confusing. Half of the pros say, "You need clips; Bite the bullet and go get them," while the other half say, "There's a way around this whole clips nonsense, and I can teach you those insider secrets."

Think of it this way: You probably would not say to your child, "Homework? Bah! I'm sure we can find a way around it." So let's just deal with clips in a practical, straightforward manner.

The basic strategy behind acquiring clips is simple: You start writing for small, local publications and work your way up to large, national, or international publications. So your progress goes something like this: 1) Write local. Use the clip and pitch regional. 2) Write regional. Use the clip and write national. 3) Write national and write for anyone you like. The essential strategy, when you're getting started, is to work your way *up* from smaller to larger publications *before* you start thinking about expanding out into diverse markets, topics, and audiences.

Clipping Strategy

If you want to get into the wider-distribution, higher-paying publications sooner rather than later, you need to be even more strategic. Here's a roundup of where to get the clips likely to impress editors.

Daily Newspapers

Newspapers are a great choice for getting clips. For one thing, the dailies usually work with freelancers, and they need a lot of content to keep their pages full. Also, newspaper editors will push you to adapt a journalistic writing style, which can improve your writing skills and help you become more professional and versatile. And unlike weekly or monthly newspapers, most daily newspapers like *The Oregonian* or the *Chicago Sun-Times* or the *Boston Globe* consistently produce a quality product. This means you will net a high-quality clip for your hard work. If you find a daily newspaper for which you feel an affinity, then this is definitely the best place to start, as all daily newspapers cover a wide variety of news and lifestyle issues. Assuming you can match the paper's tone and style, offer to work for the editor in charge of your local section, then work your way up from there. Or, if you have expertise with a particular audience—such as business, cooking, or health—approach the editor of the corresponding section.

Your Best Bet: Start by pitching one idea and try to develop a regular writing gig. Many of my students over the years have aspired to column writing. This is a fine long term goal, but columnists at the dailies are usually seasoned journalists who have paid their dues. My suggestion is to put column writing aside initially, and ask your editor where he can use you based on your strengths. You're likely to cover "a beat," which is one area or subject. Even if you start with something that doesn't interest you much, like "recreation" or "business" topics, that foot in the door can lead to better assignments down the road. Of course, newspapers don't pay as much as magazines, but when you have regular assignments, the steady money adds up. That's a free education and expense money all rolled into one.

National Trade Magazines

In addition to the national, glossy magazines at your local newsstand or bookstore, there's a whole other world of magazines you may not know about—trade journals. Trade journals are published for an audience of professionals, who

Clipping Success

- Getting clips is about the quality of each clip, not the sheer quantity you can rack up. "Quality" refers to the total value of the clip in terms of the overall package: how well it's written, edited, and designed on the page. So improve your writing skills. Editors want to work with writers who produce quality work no matter what the size and reach of their publication.

- When a clip you've worked hard for disappoints, don't be so quick to blame it on the editor or publication. Consider your role in the process before deciding not to work with an editor and publisher again. There are enough professional publishers and editors out there that there is no reason to settle for anything less.

- Offering photos with your writing for local publications can increase your paycheck— sometimes dramatically.

- Total pay divided by how many hours it takes you to write and revise the article equals how much you're making per hour. Freelancer Abigail Green keeps close track of her hourly rate. If she can write more quickly for a regional, her hourly rate is often higher than it would be writing for a national. If you can write more swiftly for regional publications and meet their editorial needs with ease, pay attention to the math. Another way Green increases her paycheck is by including national sources in regional articles. This way she can tie a local piece into a national trend and amplify its resale potential for other markets.

- Take on repeat assignments from reputable editors who want to retain you after you do a good job for them, but only until or while you continue to work on landing better-paying gigs (assuming that's your ultimate goal).

- Become a weekly correspondent (a person who reports on local news and happenings) for your daily paper from your neighborhood or town. Or contribute regularly to a quality regional magazine that reflects one of your specialties (parenting, health and wellness, fitness, food, spirituality, or pets). Regular writing assignments carried out conscientiously prepare you for working with national editors.

subscribe to stay current on trends and news specific to their industry. Think *Massage Magazine*, *Bee Culture*, and *Pizza Today*. Don't turn up your nose at the mention of trade magazines. If you haven't yet written for a national audience, your ticket to that clip may be writing for the trades. Besides, you will learn about zooming in on the mindset and needs of a specific interest group, which is great practice. Another plus: Trade magazine editors are hungry for well-written content. The pay can be anywhere from poor to very good, and if you follow through with a well-executed article, the opportunity for repeat gigs is high. However, like writing for newspapers, writing for the trades may lead you down roads that have less to do with your imagined specialty and more to do with honing your writing skills. Whether writing for the trades is your final destination or your stepping stone, it will help you acquire the all-important clips that could land you better-exposure gigs in the future.

Your Best Bet: Look at your four best audiences. Any connections between them and trade publication audiences? For example, Emmis Publishing publishes both *Country Sampler* magazine and *Country Business* magazine. Since I like writing profiles and writing about home décor, they both are a good fit for me. Go to the sites of some of your favorite magazine publishers and see what else they publish. You just might find some trades you've never heard of before that you'd enjoy writing for.

Custom and Closed-Circulation Publications

Custom publications are magazines and newsletters published by and for organizations that want a professional print media presence for business members, customers, or clients of the parent company. For example, the California State Automobile Association publishes *Via*; the Smithsonian publishes *Smithsonian*; and Costco publishes *Costco Connection*. Alumni magazines are a great choice for beginning freelancers. Writer mama Abigail Green says alumni magazines will often give an unpublished writer an assignment if she's an alum and that some of her nicest clips come from such publications. Closed-circulation magazines are aimed at readers with specific needs like *Arthritis Today*, or *bp* for people with bipolar disorder.

Your Best Bet: Order and study these publications based on your areas of interest, personal challenges, and best-bet audiences. For example, *Autism-Asperger's Digest* magazine might be a good target for a writer mama with a child who has been diagnosed with one of these conditions.

Online Markets That Pay

You can find online publications that pay by checking WritersMarket.com. Some print publications take submissions for online use only, and these are excellent choices for beginners. Avoid any online start-ups, shady deals, or editors who try to coax you in by saying they *might* pay in the future.

When clips are what you're after, focus less on how much online publications pay than on the quality of clip you'll get for your effort. However, avoid writing for any online publications for free, unless you're doing it as a promotion strategy, not a writing-business-builder strategy. The exception to this rule is if you're writing for a site with name recognition and a proven track record of professionalism and high-quality content. Bluesuitmom.com would be an example: They don't pay anymore (they used to), but they have high editorial standards and a good reputation.

Your Best Bet: Beware of wasting too much time on the hunt for online paying markets. A "quick" search on the Internet can cost you hours with no real progress made. Find references by word of mouth and through reputable writer-market providers or fellow writers.

Glossy Regional or Local Publications

There has been a proliferation of local and regional publication start-ups in recent years. For example, when I moved away from Bellingham, Washington a couple years ago, a new glossy (a magazine printed on coated paper so it appears glossy) called *Entertainment News Northwest* started up. Several of my former students now contribute to it regularly. Though the pay is in the low range, they appreciate the steady work and the high-quality clips. If and when the time is right, they can move up the pay scale by leveraging the quality clips they've acquired to expand into higher-circulation publications. Many, if not most, freelancers continue to work with regional and national publications even after they have broken in to the nationals.

Your Best Bet: If all of your time is eaten up writing for lower-paying publications, you might find yourself without enough energy to break in to higher-paying publications. Remember that "breaking out" of the groove you're comfortable in often temporarily requires a burst of energy until

✎ Portfolio Power

One of the best ways to motivate yourself is to start a portfolio of your published clips. Begin with a three-ring binder (this can be as basic or fancy as you want) and challenge yourself to see how quickly you can fill it with articles carrying your byline.

Another way to stay motivated is to have a Portfolio Party with a writer friend. Get together quarterly for coffee or lunch and toast each other's success. There's no better way to reward yourself than to share your success with someone who knows how challenging it is to get, and stay, motivated. You can even have a Portfolio Party while the kids are having a play date—a fun way to combat the usual isolation of the writing process. If the kids are very young, you can take turns watching them and perusing each other's portfolios. And while you're swapping insights into editorial likes and dislikes (this comes up naturally as part of the conversation), why not share writer's guidelines you've accumulated? A cooperative, rather than competitive, attitude will help increase both your sales.

you've "broken in" to the next level. Allow yourself to have too much work temporarily by retaining your lower paying publications while you approach higher paying markets. Eventually you'll be in the position where you need to drop your lowest paying publication in order to manage your workload. (See Wendy Burt's Accountability Sheet on pages 199–200).

Local and Regional Newspapers

These publications are generally scraping the bottom of the barrel in terms of pay, and yet they still offer some of the most creative, opinion-oriented, and colorful writing opportunities. If this interests you and you need clips, and you find a paper in which the editors do a careful and conscientious job, go ahead and write a couple articles for them, and then move on. While writing for local and regional newspapers will drain your valuable time and energy in the long run, enjoy the additional creative license they may offer for a brief interlude, and then, if breaking into the nationals is one of your goals, say, "Next!"

Your Best Bet: Local and regional newspapers sometimes can't afford professional photographers, so build up your small paycheck by offering photos with your writing. One writer mama found that she actually made more money from her photos than from her articles even though the photos took a fraction of the time and she had no professional photography experience

In the next chapter, you will learn how to submit your writing with a cover letter, and in section III, how to write a query letter to an editor to pitch (propose) your article ideas. So keep your clips handy and ready to submit as clean photocopies (for mail) or scanned PDF files posted on a Web site to which you can provide a link (for e-mail submissions).

Collect Sample Copies of Hard-to-Find Publications

Don't settle for the publications you can find locally if writing nationally is what you really want. One reason that trade, custom, and closed-circulation magazines offer more opportunities for freelancers is that you usually cannot just pick them up at your local drugstore, library, or newsstand. Chances are good that you will need to order sample issues of these publications. Although many don't charge for sample issues, determine which publications best suit your audiences before ordering. (In the case of newspapers, you will choose the section of the paper that best suits your audience.) List publications in each category below that you could and would like to write for:

Daily Newspapers, Your Best-Bet Sections:

Trade Magazines, Your Best-Bet Audiences:

Custom and Closed-Circulation Publications, Your Challenges, Interests, and Audiences:

You'll find ordering information on WritersMarket.com, or contact the publisher directly following an Internet search. Is it worth a few bucks to purchase sample copies of higher-paying publications if it increases your likelihood of landing an assignment? You bet!

Gather Every Afternoon Moment

If you are a mom, you know how to reprioritize, punt, and juggle—often simultaneously. Even if afternoon is not your first choice for writing time, this is the time of day that often, mercifully, includes naptime, which can allow even the busiest mom to jot a few thoughts on paper. While some moms use naptime to relax and recharge, writing moms reach for their pen, or streamline the rest of their day so they have time in the evening to write. Here are some tricks to have ready:

- Toddlers can be notoriously slow eaters. If you are "blessed" with a poky or a picky one, make use of the time you spend sitting at the kitchen table. Keep a notepad handy, so you can pull it out after you serve lunch and brainstorm while the kids eat.

- If you have kids of various ages at home, lunchtime is probably not going to yield any literary breakthroughs. However, if you spend your time wisely at lunch, you can earn time before or after dinner when back-up help (spouse or an older child) returns. So go ahead and set the table for dinner after lunch, get the recipes and ingredients out for dinner, and, if possible, get a jumpstart on preparation while everyone is still finishing their meal.

- If you are a really lucky writer mama, your child's naps afford you valuable extra work time. If not all your children are still in the naptime stage, you can maximize your naptime minutes by declaring afternoon Quiet Time for all your children, for as long as the napping child will sleep. During Quiet Time all children must go to their rooms, play quietly, and leave mommy alone—unless it's urgent, of course. Discourage interruptions that aren't absolutely necessary.

- Sometimes naptime gets the ax so kids can have earlier bedtimes at night. Don't let anyone guilt-trip you about what time your child goes to bed. Do what works for you and your child. You're a working writer and you need to get your work done. So if the afternoon is your best time to work, let your children take long naps and send them to bed at eight, nine, or even ten if you want.

- Try "un-napping," a trick I've learned over the years that works like a charm for a mom who needs to reboot her brain. After the kids are down for their naps, lie flat on your back, close your eyes, and rest for just a minute. Set a timer nearby to wake you in ten minutes so you won't fall into a deep sleep. Now here's the trick: Start counting down from one hundred to zero. Visualize each number as you mentally think it. You'll be "asleep" before you know it. But don't stay asleep. Get up in ten minutes. Believe it or not, you'll be refreshed and ready to work. At the very least, you'll feel more rested than you did before you un-napped.

- Afternoons are a great time to connect with other writer mamas. Maybe their kids are napping too. Write a few quick, supportive e-mails. Call a writer mama friend or offer to read and review a friend's writing during this otherwise sluggish time. It's a good warm-up before you plunge back into your own writing.

- Attend to your office duties in the afternoon. Update your Rolodex. Straighten up the paperwork on your desk. Set some quick goals. File drafts and create new folders. Do anything that will make you feel ready to write next time you sit down. Clear those decks!

6

Connect With Cover Letters

> *I submitted my article to a homeschooling magazine that rejected it immediately. I turned it right around and submitted it to a bigger magazine, not expecting a lot. The owner/editor had the article bought, the contract sent, and the check in the mail in the blink of an eye.*
>
> ~ JOHANNAH BANHAM, MOTHER OF TWELVE

There are two kinds of letters you will use to submit work as a freelance writer: cover letters and query letters. This chapter focuses on the cover letters you will write and send along with your list articles, how-tos, fillers, and essays; an abbreviated version of a cover letter will even be sent with your tips. (By contrast, query letters are sent as part of package to pitch an idea, rather than accompanied by a complete piece of writing. These will be covered in section III.) When you send your writing with a cover letter, it's a sign of your professionalism, so it's a crucial skill if you want to see your writing in print.

Write Cover Letters

At this point, you need to know when it's appropriate to send a cover letter to accompany writing that will be described in the next section.

Send your submission with a cover letter if ...

- You've checked the writer's guidelines and the publication accepts unsolicited manuscripts (unsolicited means the editor did not explicitly request it); *and*
- You have written a piece that perfectly matches (not "kind of" matches) the tone, style, subject matter, and audience of the publication; *and*
- You are certain that your article fits, in terms of word count, in a specific section of the publication.

Don't send your submission with a cover letter if ...

- You have never read or studied the publication to determine if your article is a good fit. Generally, you must study several issues of the publication and double-check the latest issue to ensure that the magazine has not been reformatted in any drastic ways; *or*

- You have an *idea* for an article, not a completed article. That's appropriate for a query letter, not a cover letter; *or*
- The publication doesn't accept unsolicited manuscripts, but does accept queries from new writers. (Check the guidelines to find out if this is the case. See chapters fourteen and fifteen on query writing.)

The Cover Letter Demystified

Cover letters seem straightforward until you try to write one. Then you realize you have to cram an awful lot of only the most pertinent information into one page. If you've struggled with cover letter writing in the past, don't feel bad. Writing a good, solid cover letter is a skill you develop with practice. Tighten your sentences until they are crisp and succinct and follow these suggestions:

Paragraph One: Connect with your editor. Moms know that a sincere compliment goes a long way. So start your cover letter with a little editor appreciation:

- What do you notice or like about the publication?
- What topics do you find compelling or interesting?
- Does the magazine accomplish its mission?

The compliment is not intended to snow editors. A good editor can tell the difference between a genuine compliment and baloney. There are also a few things an editor needs to know, right off the bat: namely, whether you are a subscriber; and if not, how familiar you are with the publication. Communicate convincingly that you have taken time out of your busy schedule to read their publica-

Keep Your Submissions in Circulation

Writer mama C. Hope Clark has a great rule of thumb to keep her submissions in the hands of editors and not on her hard drive: She keeps thirteen submissions circulating at any one time. Her motto, "Keep thirteen in play," serves as a reminder of her golden rule. Most successful writers use a similar strategy whereby they immediately resubmit rejected manuscripts somewhere else in order to keep finished writing "in play."

Track your submissions by setting up a simple spreadsheet like Hope does. If you don't have a spreadsheet program, you can always use the table feature in your word-processing program. Down the left-hand column, list your article titles. And across the top, use the following labels: Title; Publisher; Date Sent; Follow-Up Date; Payment; Notes.

After you submit your writing, simply fill in the relevant details on your spreadsheet and make a note on your calendar to follow up after the requested consideration time has expired.

If Editor Number One rejects your initial submission, or you simply never hear from him, send him two more submissions in hopes of breaking through. If you hear nothing after three attempts, move him to the bottom of your priority list. If it's a publication you really want to break into, revisit the writer's guidelines or masthead every six months, because editorial changes happen frequently. When an editorial change happens, begin submitting again. Two places to stay current on industry news are www.woodenhorsepub.com and www.writers-

tion closely. Nothing turns off an editor faster than a fly-by-night freelancer who is just trying to place articles and hasn't bothered to read the publication, and who makes that obvious in a cover letter. Seriously, put yourself in the editor's shoes. Why should he give you an assignment if you haven't even bothered to read the magazine?

Paragraph Two: Explain why your submission is a good match. Don't expect that your editor will be so eager to read your manuscript that taking the time to summarize the pertinent details in the cover letter is unnecessary. The purpose of your cover letter is to briefly give the information that tells the editor, at a glance, whether your manuscript is worth looking over. If it doesn't do the job, don't be surprised if your manuscript gets tossed into the recycle bin. Here are some key points to make in the cover letter:

- Is your piece written in a tone, style, or voice consistent with other articles?
- Is your piece on a topic the publication frequently covers? Do you have more info, newer info, a fresh take or an opposite take on the topic?
- Are you a known expert with depth of insight to offer, or have you interviewed known experts?
- Are you providing the right information at the right time (a connection to the season or current events)?

Paragraph Three: What's the article? At a glance, here's what your editor wants to know. (And she's gaining speed as she reads, so keep it short and sweet.)

- What's the title of your submission? (Match it to those in the magazine.)
- What form of article is it (how-to, list, profile, etc.)? (Make it one they run.)
- How long is it? (Use your word count tool and make sure it fits within their standards.)
- How is it similar, yet different, to something they've recently published? (Compare/contrast.)

Paragraph Four: Why should she publish you? There are really only two answers to this question: 1) You are a reputable, professional freelance journalist with an established track record; or 2) You are a beginning freelancer who is conscientious and flexible. The fourth paragraph is called the bio paragraph, and it improves and evolves the more you publish. Not to be confused with your entire résumé or curriculum vitae, this paragraph should include only your relevant writing and publishing experience. Leave everything else, including what credentials you *don't* have, out. If you want to beef up your bio, send out more submissions!

In your bio, be sure to include that you are a freelance journalist (just say "yes"); where, what, and how much you have published (leave out anything not relevant); and what makes you more knowledgeable than the average person on this topic (mention personal or professional experience, more on expertise in chapter twenty).

Here is the bio a former student of mine used to accompany a personal essay on the topic of autism for *Brain, Child* magazine. Note how she highlights her status as a person with relevant personal experience and leaves it at that.

I am a freelance writer from Holliston, Massachusetts. In addition to being Sam's mother, I serve as the only parent member on our school district's "Exploring the Options" team, a group of

First Impressions Go a Long Way: Check Covers Twice

Of course, your letter and manuscript should be as error-free as possible. Here's a checklist to help you avoid common errors:

- ❏ Are the editor's name and position and the title of the publication and address correct?
- ❏ Did you use a standard business letter format for snail mail or standard business e-mail format (more on this topic on pages 170–171)?
- ❏ Did you read your letter out loud a couple of times to make sure you don't trip over your words?
- ❏ Did you run your spelling and grammar check and look up any exceptions or questions in your stylebook? Remember, spell-check won't catch errors like "there" for "their."
- ❏ Did you proof your letter twice and have another pair of eyes also proof it at least once?

Then send that puppy out!

educators and administrators charged with providing support and guidance to the district's autism specialist.

That's all you need to do! Keep your cover letter simple and to the point, and let your strong manuscript speak for itself. If the editor likes your article, if it is a good fit with her audience and editorial needs, and if she has an opening, she will publish it. The editor may also request to keep your submission on file until there is an opening, in which case you should ask how long she wishes to hold it, and then follow up when that time has expired. At that point, if the editor cannot commit to publishing your piece, you should resubmit it elsewhere.

The Freelance Three-Step

To increase your chances of successfully placing work you have already written for publication, you will need to find a cover letter writing-and-submitting rhythm that works for you. Here are three steps you will want to include:

1. Submit. Once you complete the exercises in the next section, you will have several manuscripts to submit. Your goal is to get your manuscript into those tall piles on every editorial assistant's desk. So forget being flashy or using gimmicks; just write well and get your work out there!
2. Follow up. Often, you won't hear back from an editor after you make a submission. That's why you need to designate two days out of the month as "follow-up days." On follow-up days, you revisit your submissions (I suggest you use one folder in which you keep all your outstanding submissions for sanity's sake), skim what you've sent, and determine which submissions have "expired"—meaning the editor has had them as long as outlined in the guidelines and you haven't heard back.

Send a brief e-mail regarding your expired submissions, stating what you sent and when, and a polite inquiry asking if the editor is interested. If you don't hear back within a week, the editor is not interested.

3. **Move on or celebrate, but keep submitting.** Above all, when it comes to submitting your writing, stay detached and move onto your next project. You are learning by improving your writing and submitting skills as you go. Do not obsess about what an editor thinks about one submission. Your goal is to have numerous submissions out for consideration at one time. If you receive a rejection or no response to a follow-up, use the "twenty-four-hour rule." Give yourself a day to feel however you feel, and then get that sucker resubmitted to another editor.

And when you get an acceptance, celebrate for a day and then leverage that wave of confidence into getting your previously rejected or ignored submissions back into the game. See how it works?

What's Already on Your Hard Drive?

Comb through your hard drive; check your notes and your journal. What have you got that could be quickly polished and submitted? In as matter-of-fact a manner as you can muster, gather the writing, polish the writing, submit the writing, track the writing, and then ask, "What's next?" Your ability to submit your work is, without question, crucial to your livelihood. If you don't submit, you don't make money. It's that simple. Like everything else, if you focus on the little steps, you'll eventually get the hang of it.

exercise

Wring Every Second From the Evenings

The evenings can be a great time to work on your writing.

No really; I'm not joking! If you have older kids, they likely have homework. If they are old enough to work independently, you can work while they work. Or, if they are younger, they may have practices, Girl Scouts, or other activities that allow you some quiet time. If you have very young children, chances are they go to bed fairly early, which can open up your evening hours. Take advantage of these moments whenever they present themselves. Here are some suggestions for making your evenings more productive when you need to find more writing time:

- If you are already a night owl, go ahead and take that daily nap during the afternoon so you'll have more energy in the evening. Just crash with your kids, or find a resting spot within earshot of their stirring. You'll be more energized in the evenings even if you don't actually fall asleep.

- If you're not a night owl, you may be tired after dinner and just want to get to your desk and get your work over with, but a fifteen-minute power walk around the block, a quick dance, or big stretch will help you revitalize your body and mind so you can work more efficiently. It will improve your mood, as well.

- Once you sit down, try setting a timer for twenty minutes and doing something easy or fun right off the bat. Write a funny anecdote from your day, or rough out an inspirational article—go in a direction that feels easiest for you or that you associate with warming up. Then, when the timer rings, you'll be ready to grind out some nitty-gritty research for an article or edit the draft of your personal essay for the zillionth time.

- When the sitcom laughter from another room starts to lure you away from your work, grab your timer again, but this time for the tough stuff. Here's how it works: Respond to e-mails—twenty minutes, go! Draft an article—twenty minutes, go! Proofread yesterday's draft—twenty minutes, go! Plan for next week—twenty minutes, go! You can get a lot done in short bursts if you practice working that way.

- Of course, some mamas may not be able to squeeze much time from their days, so don't completely rule out writing late at night. Novelist and writer mama Heather Sharfeddin awoke in the middle of the night with the idea for her first published novel, *Blackbelly*. Fortunately, she'd been dealing with insomnia long enough to already be in the habit of shuffling to her computer, where she'd write until sleep beckoned her back to bed. For some mamas, late-night hours are the best you can get. But hey, you can still make it work. Just be sure to get the rest you need to function the next morning.

II.
Practice

7

Tip Off Everyone

> *Everyone who is published was once unpublished.*
> *You really have to believe in yourself and build*
> *yourself up instead of worrying that you're not*
> *good enough.*
>
> ~ BARBARA DeMARCO-BARRETT, MOTHER OF ONE

The basic rhythm of writing and submitting your work can be learned from the tiniest form of paid writing: tips. Not all publications pay for tips, but some, like those that fall under the parenting and women's categories, often do. Sometimes jotting a five-sentence tip onto paper is about as much as a mom can handle on a hectic day, so that makes it a great place to start. One tiny tip submission is better than saving up your big ideas for "someday" and never getting around to submitting them.

What is a tip? A tip is a solution to a problem addressed to an audience that will appreciate it. Easy, right? That's all there is to it—just a helpful suggestion from one person's experience for the benefit of another person. If you start looking at what you already read, you will notice, using your "tip-ray vision," that tips are practically omnipresent.

Can you write and submit tips for publication? Yes, you can! Here's a tip I had published in the May 2006 issue of *Parents* Magazine:

> ### Great Shakes
>
> My 3-year-old daughter, Samantha Rose, loves fruit but never finishes the whole banana or pear. I hate wasting food, so I rinse any leftovers and pop them into a freezer bag. When she wants a smoothie, we're ready to go with a variety of frozen fruits.
>
> —CHRISTINA KATZ; WILSONVILLE, ORE.

I realize it's not *Wuthering Heights*, but the point is that a tip is nothing more than a few sentences in response to a problem (my daughter is a picky eater and doesn't finish her food) that offers a solution (put leftover fruit in a freezer bag and make smoothies out of it).

Tips Q&A

Q: Can I make up tips?

A: Better not. Without real-life experience behind your tips, they won't ring true. Sure, you can exaggerate ideas slightly, but don't fabricate them completely. An important lesson to learn early is that fictionalizing nonfiction material is unprofessional and unethical. If you need to amplify an idea, go ahead, but don't make up stuff. It might become a habit.

Q: There are many requests for tips out there. Can't I just submit my tips for free?

A: Writing a free tip—or article for that matter—is not going to derail your career. In fact, if you have nothing else going on, writing for free can prime the pump. In general, however, writing for free is best for getting started or making a charitable contribution.

You will often encounter the should-I-write-for-free question when you begin to submit your writing. Remember, you will never run out of opportunities to write for free. Why not practice taking a few extra steps right now to identify publications that pay for tips?

Q: Okay, so where can I get a complete listing of publications that publish tips?

A: Nowhere. The point is: Tips are for readers. You need to actually read a magazine to qualify to submit a tip. That's the deal. That's why they are called "tips from our readers." So you probably won't want to submit tips unless you are, or plan to become, a reader. When seeking tip opportunities, check parenting, women's, pregnancy, bridal, cooking, and craft publications (just to name a few) for opportunities that either pay or offer alternative compensation. Some publications, like *Fit Pregnancy*, offer products valuing between twenty and ninety dollars in exchange for tips. Others, like *Budget Travel*, offer a subscription in exchange for one publishable tip. Some editors invite photos to accompany tips. But always be sure to read the fine print: Many cooking publications will take your recipes, tips, and photos and offer you nada in return.

Brainstorm Some Tip Ideas

To help you get started, here are some tip categories I gleaned from already-published tips in *Parents* magazine, and a few ideas I brainstormed.

Rituals

Problem: Difficulty with transitions

Solution: Sing "The Bye-Bye Song."

Hygiene

Problem: Challenges of brushing toddler's teeth

Solution: Play "Find the sugar bugs."

Eating

Problem: Picky eater

Solution: Introduce new foods often, and offer them at least three times in a row.

Manners

Problem: Child forgets manners at home (but uses them everywhere else)

Solution: Model the way we'd like her to speak and respond.

Potty Training

Problem: Delayed interest in potty training

Solution: Use star chart for rewards; treats are earned for accumulated stars.

Tantrums

Problem: Tantrum escalates quickly once started

Solution: Act silly to circumvent child's tantrum. Take feeling (frustration, anger or whatever) and act it out in an exaggerated manner.

How to Submit Your Tips

Being a magazine's reader is the only requirement for submitting tips. Writing reader tips is good practice for the future, when you will pitch longer pieces for publication. Just be sure to work with a magazine that actually publishes tips. For this example, let's stick with *Parents*, since I've already mentioned it. *Parents* pays twenty-five dollars for tips from readers in the "It Worked for Me!" section. It lists the e-mail address for submissions right after the list of tips: You can address your e-mail to "Dear It Worked For Me Editor." Simply state that you are a reader and you'd like to offer a tip or two. It's best to offer one or two tips rather than deluge the editor with too many ideas at once; also, one concise tip is preferable to several rambling, half-thought-out ideas. This applies to everything you write and submit.

Tip Clipboards

Keep tip lists around the house so you can track your ideas as they come to you: inside the kitchen and bathroom cupboards, on a clipboard by the family bulletin board, by the phone, inside a handy drawer, near places you do

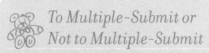

To Multiple-Submit or Not to Multiple-Submit

Should you send a tip you write for one parenting magazine to several others? I don't recommend it. Instead of doing that, it's better to practice being responsive, and customize each tip to each specific magazine. In *Parents*, tip topics revolve around parenting younger children. In comparison, pick up *Family Fun* (they pay one hundred dollars for their tips). Their topics are for school-age children: organizing toys, family-friendly ways to grocery shop, how to handle a move, family games, and holiday décor. Compare and contrast the tip sections of the two magazines to discern how each targets its readership. Tips may differ in tone, length, and topic, as well as audience. They are customized to the specific reader demographics, which is why even two parenting magazines can be very different.

repetitive tasks (like the laundry room or next to the dishwasher), and in your bedside table drawer.

Develop Your Ideas

After closely reading a current issue of *Parents*, pick whichever of your ideas feels the most fresh, without being too outrageous or over-the-top. Here's what I might submit in hopes of catching a young assistant editor's eye, since that's who usually makes the selections:

> My four-year-old, Samantha Rose, doesn't have tantrums often, but when she does it's impossible to redirect her. So now as soon as a tantrum kicks off, I pick up on her strongest feeling (anger, frustration, sadness, etc.) and exaggerate it into monster-sized proportions. Then, while playing the part of The Tantrum Monster, I show her how silly a tantrum looks by pounding pillows or kicking my arms and legs while lying face down on the bed. Naturally, I don't do this in public. But at home, the Tantrum Monster can break the tension, spark some laughs, and make the difference between a learning opportunity and a total blowout.

Your tips will usually be between 50 and 100 words after you've edited them. At 108 words, this tip is a tad long, but not overly so. As with any of your writing accepted for publication, your editor will tighten it up and edit for length. And there's no shame in being edited—that's what editors are paid to do!

Tips are short exercises in brief, crisp writing that are quick, fun, and gratifying to submit, as well as excellent warm-ups for the longer, more complicated forms you will tackle as your writing career progresses.

Submit Your Tips

Write and submit tips to magazines that fall under your four best audiences list (from chapter two). Compare two publications within the same audience category at a time so you can learn how magazines that seem similar at first glance are actually very targeted. The only way to understand how target audience directly affects editorial content is by closely comparing and contrasting the writing. Beginners who have trouble writing to suit a target audience will have trouble breaking in, even when writing super-short pieces like tips. So don't miss this opportunity to really "get" the concept of target audience. By the time you are finished, you will be able to easily pick up on subtle differences from here on.

exercise

Stake Out Spaces and Start a Wishlist

As your career grows you will need to claim more space for your work. The kitchen table works well for journaling, the couch for reading, the dining room for spreading out notes for rough drafts, the computer is ideal for revising and polishing. Sometimes it's best to leave the house altogether and head for the nearest library or café, so you can get away from it all and concentrate. Think of your search for space as a grand experiment, and as you discover what works, stake it off temporarily—or permanently—from the rest of the family, and see how that goes. If you find yourself breathing a sigh of relief, you're on the right track.

WORKPLACE NUMBER ONE: A QUIET SPOT WHERE YOU CAN CONCENTRATE

I recently moved my office from a 10 x 10 bedroom to one twice as large. It seems natural to allow my writing space to expand alongside my career. However, along the way I have written in bathrooms while my daughter was sleeping, at a desk or a computer set up in the dining area, even at a desk in a closet, for privacy. There is no "wrong" place to write, so long as you can create a quiet spot to call your own. This is the place you will get the bulk of your work done because as soon as you sit down your space reminds you that you are a professional. And this is where you do the work that makes the money to contribute to your family's income, so take it seriously.

WORKPLACE NUMBER TWO: THE COMPUTER

No doubt you will end up working wherever your computer is set up. So consider whether your current computer setup works for you. You may need to negotiate with your spouse and kids as to who gets to use the computer and when. I suggest you either set up regular times for each family member or try the sign-up sheet system used at libraries. In the long run, however, you should have computer of your own.

WORKPLACE NUMBER THREE: ANYWHERE BUT HOME

Get the heck out of Dodge, whenever necessary and possible, in order to be more productive. I've worked everywhere from my parked car to a park bench, and sometimes I take my notepad for walks in a fit of "I've gotta get outta here!" The to-go bag is a key to your sanity and productivity, and will come to your emotional rescue whether your destination is the nearest public library, quiet café, or bookstore where you can sit comfortably and work. If you are going to write away from home, you"ll need:

- a tote bag with plenty of room
- a handful of retractable pens that won't leak
- a notepad for writing
- a smaller notepad for taking notes, making lists, and jotting down ideas
- sticky notes for marking pages
- whatever folder of writing you are currently working on
- a laptop and carrying case (if you use one)

THE WISH LIST

Every week (or every day) you will stumble across items—supplies, books, e-books, and classes—you are convinced you cannot live without. The best place for these is on your Wish List. Here's why: What you *need* when you're getting started is a blank piece of paper or clean screen, a target market to aim for, and motivation. That's pretty much it. Anything else is making things more complicated than you have time for just yet.

Over time, your workload will increase as your career grows. You will eventually want to expand further, which may involve classes, books, association memberships, and the like. For now, however, make do with what you have, and park your Wish List in a place that's accessible, but where it won't distract you from the work at hand. Ask for Wish List items as birthday and holiday gifts—you can even set up a registry-type list through Amazon.com. Over the years, you can build a respectable reference library from scratch, as I have. Here are some great items to put on your wish list:

- laptop computer (new, used, refurbished, or hand-me-down)
- *Writer's Market* (the latest edition by Writer's Digest Books)
- *Formatting and Submitting Your Manuscript* (Writer's Digest Books)
- inspirational writing books
- writing reference books (see appendix)
- writing how-to books for nonfiction writers and freelancers and on book proposal writing

NO EARNINGS, NO SHOPPING, SISTER!

If you love to shop, try limiting supply shopping to bulk orders on a quarterly rotation. This helps train you to base your quarterly spending (how much you can reinvest back in your business) on your quarterly earnings, which will only motivate you to write and submit more work.

P.S. Your significant other will like this idea too.

8

List Your Way Into Print

> *Writing brings out the best in me. My children can tell you that their mother is a much better person as a writing mom than just earning bacon for the table. It's a win-win situation for the family and for me.*
>
> ~ C. Hope Clark, mother of two

L ist articles are fun, easy to write, and always in demand. Just as they sound, the organizational principle in a list article is a series of tips, anecdotes, or examples organized around a particular theme. Anyone who has ever stood in a checkout line has seen a list article: "12 Ways to Look Younger Today!" or "6 Secrets for Keeping the Love Alive in your Marriage!" Even television has its version of list articles. Take for example, the David Letterman Top Ten List. Who decides the order? Dave. How does he decide? It has everything to do with being hilarious to his late-night television demographic. (Even Dave has to think about his audience. At least his writers do.)

A good time to try your hand at list articles is when you see a published list article and think, "I could have written that!" Well, don't just say or think it; prove it! You can brainstorm your own lists and submit them with a cover letter (when asked for in the guidelines). Otherwise, in section three, you'll learn how to query to place your list article, by extracting the strongest elements from your list-in-progress and including them in a pitch. To get you started, take your tip ideas and expand them into list articles. You'll be publishing them painlessly in no time, and could continue publishing list articles as long as you like.

To get in the mood, check out these recent list article titles spotted on the newsstand:

"36 Speed Cleaning Tricks"—*Women's Day*

"10 Deadly Health Habits You Must Fix Today"—*Redbook*

"Our 12 Favorite Chocolate Desserts"—*Good Housekeeping*

"6 Ways to Feel Closer to Your Husband"—*Parenting*

"Best Ways to Dump the Stress and Feel Happier"—*Parents*

"12 Ways to Reduce Your Risk of Pre-Term Birth"—*Pregnancy*

And don't be fooled by a list article just because it doesn't have a number in the title. "The best way," "a new way," or doing things "better" are common list article devices.

Want to know why else a mom would want to write list articles? Here are seven good reasons:

1. List articles are everywhere. The tagline for Wordstock, a local book festival in Portland, Oregon, is: "Change me, book. Please. Do it." Alter that slightly to "Change me, list article. Please. Do it. *And hurry up, I don't have much time!*" and you will understand, in a nutshell, why readers love information presented in list form.

Need proof? Hit the newsstands. What kind of article do you see on magazine covers more than any other? List articles. Editors love list articles precisely because readers love list articles. Readers can scan a list on the run to glean ways to change or improve their busy lives.

Even books are written in list format: Dr. Stephen Covey's *The Seven Habits of Highly Effective People*, for example.

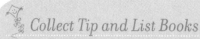

Collect Tip and List Books

If you have topics or audiences you write for over and over, see if you can't find a book of tips on that topic or for that audience to keep yourself rolling. There's nothing like reading some well-written list articles to spark more ideas. Let's say you like to write parenting tips—did you know magazines occasionally publish entire books of parenting tips? Check out *The Parents Book of Lists* (lists *and* tips) or *Family Circle's 2000 Hints and Tips: For Cooking, Cleaning, Organizing, and Simplifying Your Life*. It has lists of tips for parents that are not only handy but can jog your brain into cranking out some lists of your own.

And if you want to make your list articles juicier, pick up a copy of the *The New Book of Lists: The Original Compendium of Curious Information* by David Wallenchinsky and Amy Wallace. You will be amazed by the number of tips you can generate on one topic. Possibly enough for a list book of your own one day!

Holy Paper Overload, Mama!

Yup, it's true. You will go through paper like crazy. Worse, you will be constantly collecting paper in the forms of newspapers, magazines, and journals, so you can consider writing for them. How in the world are you going to manage all this paper? By using systems that you customize. (And by conducting a quarterly paper purge!)

Along the course of your writing career, your paper flow will get larger and larger. Though I am very fond of trees, I can't do nearly as thorough an editing job without a piece of paper in front of me. But, of all the writer mamas I talked to about managing their work and paper flow, author Sharon Cindrich said it best,: "Just like there is not one way to parent, there is no one perfect system for parent writers." As my family life and career have changed, so have my systems. Here's a list of organizational tools and systems you may find helpful:

- Plastic bins and containers (preferably totable for projects in process and flat and wide for storing extra office supplies and bulk magazines and newspapers)
- Stackable desktop folder holder—so you can see your projects in process
- Color folders—to make each assignment easy to identify
- Good, old-fashioned filing cabinets and folders—for when you want to file things away
- Cardboard or plastic magazine holders—for publications you wish to write for
- Multiple containers for separating favorite pens from junky pens, dry erase markers from regular markers, and a variety of bowls, cups, and dishes to hold miscellaneous desk supplies visible and within reach (paperclips, sticky notes, notecards, etc.)
- Bulletin boards and ephemera boards (those padded boards with ribbons criss-crossing them) for keeping track of little items that might otherwise be misplaced (business cards, thank you notes, glasses, etc.)
- A multiple-compartment paper sorter, stackable paper sorters, and storage cubes with fabric drawers (good for everything from sorting mail to papers to projects)

2. You already know how to write tips. List articles are basically a series of tips, which you already know how to write. Take a closer look at a tip you wrote (and maybe even published), and you will find a potential topic for a list article. That idea I had about making fruit smoothies with my picky-eater-daughter's leftover fruit? As a list article it could become "Seven Strategies for Dealing With Picky Eaters." The number is just a placeholder; I'll find out how many strategies there actually are, for me, after I write several drafts of the article. And I might change the number when I conduct research or add quotes.

3. List articles are easy to study and emulate. Once you find some example list articles, tear them out and put them in an accordion folder or plastic bin. This tickler file will help you warm up before you tackle a first draft. When you need inspiration for a list article, just peruse your collection. Studying sample list articles will help you catch their cadence—punchy, positive, helpful, and catchy.

4. List articles are often written by freelancers. Once you identify a publication that accepts list articles, determine if the articles are written by a freelancer or by a staff person. If you can't find the list article's byline on the masthead, you have discovered an article written by a freelancer. If an article doesn't have any byline whatsoever, it was probably generated in-house, which may mean the editor assigns freelance articles for that spot—or it may not. In other words, it's not a definite match. You don't want to waste your time on a publication that generates its list articles in-house. Stick with the best possible matches for now.

5. List articles begin off the top of your head. Here are some topics of list articles I have written recently: "12 Ways to Take Your Writing Career to the

Next Level (That Don't Involve Writing)," "10 Ways to Spring Forward in Your Writing Career," and "Summertime and the Writing Is Easy." Each is a collection of tips that match the promise of the article. List articles can, but don't necessarily need to, be in any kind of sequential order. More likely, topics within list articles are ordered based on newsworthiness (something new), relevance (to the specific audience), and freshness (for the reader). The most integrated way to pull your list together usually evolves as you go through the rewrite process.

6. Adding research to your list articles is a snap. Research, news, and trend tidbits make your tips chewier and more engaging. For example, when I was writing "Hollywood Rx for the Holidays," an article of holiday sanity tips gleaned from classic holiday movies, I chose the movies first, then the tips. Once I picked my movies, I dug deeper into each using the Internet to find plots, quotes, and trivia, until I had enough insight to uncover a tip like this one:

Detach From Family Drama

Remember Jodie Foster's 1995 film *Home for the Holidays?* The story begins with Claudia Larson (Holly Hunter) flying home to spend Thanksgiving with her wildly dysfunctional family. How many of us empathized with the family reunion drama that prompts Claudia to explain, "Nobody means what they say on Thanksgiving, Mom. You know that. That's what the day's supposed to be all about, right? Torture."

You can do the same: Come up with a list of tips any way you like and then start your research. If one doesn't pan out or you find a better one along the way, no worries. Let the final list evolve as you hunt.

7. Use personal experience to make your list articles universal. What makes a really good list article? Sharing details that bring the tip to life. Sometimes these details are personal, but in writing list articles you will learn to share specifics in a way any reader can relate to. How is this done? For "Hollywood Rx for the Holidays," I remembered that when I had a day job, I sometimes spearheaded impromptu fundraisers among co-workers. So I turned my experience into a suggestion anyone could try. You can't tell it's about me because it's addressing the reader directly. Focusing on the reader's experience rather than your own can draw her in and make her feel involved:

> Could you spearhead an impromptu fundraiser at your office or social group? You may decide to donate locally or abroad. Web resources such as www.altgifts.org or www.heiferproject.org make researching and selecting an international cause easy.

No List of Excuses

Lists are a great way to get started freelancing. In addition to the tips I've given you, don't forget to draw on the knowledge you already have just from reading list articles for years. Simply uncover the common denominator between your personal experiences and your readers, and you will find ample material for your future list articles. And there is no shortage of magazines that will publish list articles. So don't hesitate to get started listing your way into print today.

S-T-R-E-T-C-H Your Tips Into Lists

Now you are ready to write a list article of your own. Choose a tip you already wrote and expand it into a full-blown list article. Formulate your title as a question and then answer it. For example, I might ask "What are ten ways to interrupt temper tantrums before they go too far?" Off the top of your head, jot down your top ten tips. Then do a bit of research on each tip. Want to know how much research you'll need? Look at the example articles in your target publication again. (Remember to check whether they pay freelancers for list articles before you start writing!) Then estimate the ratio of suggestion to facts, figures, quotes, etc. Don't forget to use "you" statements instead of "I" statements in your later drafts to draw your reader in. It may take you a whole week to pull a list article together and tighten it to the point that it will sell. Just have fun and make it enjoyable and educational for the reader.

How to Handle Procrastination

Writing, as a process, is as simple as three steps—preparation, process, execution—but human nature makes it complicated. Add motherhood to the mix, and a simple project, like writing an article and cover letter, can easily become bogged down with our resistance, fears, and excuses. Believe me, I've heard your reasons, and they are all capable of bringing your writing to a screeching halt. Here are some strategies to get you over the hump:

Call a trusted friend or ask your spouse to "just listen" for five or ten minutes. It's amazing how you can get nearly any frustration off your chest in lightning speed when you are not interrupted. If your friend or partner is a "fixer" or "troubleshooter," give advance warning: You just need a listener, and then you'd like to get back to work. E-mail will also work in a pinch. Same caveat: No need to respond, I just need to get this off my chest so I can get back to work. I bet you do the same for others all the time.

Write about the weather. On days when my internal weather forecast is partly cloudy with showers expected by mid-morning, a half hour of journaling can wipe out those predictions and set me on a new course. Look outside your window. What's happening? That's as good a place to start writing as any.

Have other creative outlets. I make collages. Nothing fancy; more like the scrapbook's embarrassing little sister. But there is something about ripping up magazine photos into little pieces and then putting them back together in my own design that soothes me. When you think about it, it's not all that different than the writing process—and yet, because it is so visual, it relaxes my mind and helps me get back on track. Do you paint, scrapbook, knit? Any creative outlet that doesn't eat up all of your writing time can augment your writing practice.

Clear something out. I stood over our kitchen junk drawer a couple weeks ago and gained incredible satisfaction by dumping everything out and putting back in only what I really need. The rest got put away in the proper place or thrown out. As usual, when I organize something on the outside, my thoughts are more orderly afterward. When you're feeling stuck or confused, "sort it out."

Of course, if I am talking about organizing, cleaning can't be far behind. But here's the key: If you're on a deadline, keep your cleaning projects small and manageable. For example, set the timer for twenty minutes and tidy and wipe surfaces. The appearance of order will clear your mind. Or fold one batch of laundry, do a load of dishes, or clean the shower and that's it. You will emerge with your mind clean and your thoughts more clear and this will be reflected in your writing.

Find a deadline while you are waiting to land one. Take a class, call a local editor, work with a published writing partner—whatever it takes to get you focused and motivated. Funny how when a deadline is looming, you simply don't have time for procrastination. You have to dive in and get to work. Go figure.

9

Satisfy Editorial Needs With Fillers

> *I highly recommend trying your hand at fillers. They're great, easy money and you usually get paid faster than you do for longer pieces like feature articles.*
>
> ~ WENDY BURT, MOTHER OF ONE

M any moms come into my classes with dreams of publishing feature-length articles, only to be disappointed to discover how much time and energy features take to write and market from start to finish. Most editors require a query letter before they offer feature-length assignments, and these letters take practice to master (as we'll discuss in section III).

So rather than scaling two new mountains—query writing and feature writing—why not just start with one little hill? Fillers, also called shorts, are those sound-bitey pieces often collected together in the front or back of the magazine, and can be as short as a handful of sentences or as long as several paragraphs. Moms who start their careers by writing fillers become attuned to the laws of supply and demand in the writing world while learning the same skills that will help with feature writing later.

Like list articles, fillers are everywhere, with short, catchy titles such as:

"The Peril of Plastics"—*Child*

"An Animated Film for the Whole Family"—*Family Fun*

"Starring Women"—*Pink*

"Choose the Best Multivitamin"—*Cooking Light*

"Madam, Your Bath Is Ready"—*Health*

The number of filler opportunities varies among publications, and even from issue to issue. Sometimes filler opportunities outnumber feature opportunities by more than ten to one; other times, there are only a few filler opportunities in one issue. And sometimes fillers get the editorial boot when editors use reader input or promotional material for new products to cut costs. Yet some editors still want, need, and invite fillers from inexperienced writers, making fillers an excellent place to start. By the time you're ready for your

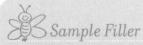 *Sample Filler*

Healthier Cooking Techniques
By Kelly James-Enger
From *McCall's* magazine, April 1999

Most of us are making an effort to eat healthier, and that usually means adding more fruits and vegetables to our daily diet. Careful, though—you may actually be sabotaging your efforts by cooking the vitamins right out of your food.

Although some nutrients are lost during the cooking and preparing process, you can minimize this by following these suggestions from registered dietitian and American Dietetic Association spokesperson Barbara Gollman:

- Don't wash produce until you're ready to eat it—fruits and vegetables contain a natural substance in their skin that helps them keep longer.
- Leave tomatoes, potatoes, and ripening fruits out but refrigerate all other produce.
- Use a vegetable brush to scrub produce under running water to remove pesticides and bacteria, but leave edible skins, which contain fiber.
- Cook or steam veggies in a covered pot or microwave them to preserve nutrients.
- When boiling veggies, bring the water to a boil before adding them. Use a small amount of water and incorporate it into your main dish.

first feature assignment, you'll be well prepared and more efficient at hunting down and using the facts, news, and trends that make fillers—and your feature articles—tick. When writing fillers, keep the following things in mind:

Forget personal pleasures; consider personal challenges. Good choices for filler topics are health, diet and fitness, mini-how-tos, breaking news, or calendar-related tie-ins. Instead of getting filler ideas from positive experiences, think of

✻ Painless Research Prompts

Just-right research. If research isn't your favorite pastime, it can be difficult to get started. Conversely, if you like research, it can be a great way to procrastinate. If you notoriously avoid researching, strike a deal with yourself like, "I will not finish this manuscript until I have found at least five facts I did not already know." Or, if you tend to overdo research, "Once I have five key facts, I will stop researching and start drafting."

Talking it out. Because research can turn into a black hole that eats up time and creates too many possible directions, chat about your topic briefly with a friend. Ask her what she thinks data resources might be. An ideal person with whom to have such a conversation is your local research librarian.

Staying focused. Don't overdo your research to the point where your writing starts to sound like a research paper. Get your line of reasoning down on paper to keep you focused and on a straight and narrow hunt.

your current life challenges. Maybe, as a sit-while-you-work writer mama, you've found yourself gaining weight. Ask yourself, "What's the latest, greatest way to address this problem?" The answer to your question would likely make a good filler of interest to millions of people who also work at home.

Conduct research quickly. Warning: It's easy to get lost in research, even when it's only for a two-hundred-word short. Remember, you're not writing a feature yet. When researching, just get in, get what you need, and get out. If you make a habit of staying on track and being efficient, you'll get the work done and be able to work just as efficiently when you graduate to feature writing. Here's how to dig for the information you'll need:

- Read recent studies, polls, or special reports
- Visit not-for-profit and research foundations online (look under "news" or "media" on their Web sites)
- Scope out medical or other kinds of journals

- Notice surprising facts (like those heard on TV or read in the newspaper) then research them further

- Interview experts for quotes from the field

- Get on lists to receive press releases sent out to attract media attention in your areas of speciality

Dig deeper, then double-size your draft. A good rule of thumb is to write twice as long as what you need (but no more), then whittle your filler down to size. Editors want fresh, newsy, and surprising fillers that will catch a reader's eye. Fillers are sound bites, so they must be flashier than longer pieces. Writer mama Kelly James-Enger says editors are looking for "a lot of information, condensed in a tight, readable form."

When it comes to fillers, fluff won't sell. Don't try to be poetic. Get straight to the point. Be a reporter. What is the gist of the story? What does the reader absolutely need to know? Start there, then simply give the key facts. Make it meaty and you'll be sure to sell it.

Practice good timing. Timing means three things when talking about fillers:

1. Tying in your filler with what's going on at the time it will be published

2. Making sure your submission lands in an editor's inbox at the best possible time to get picked up

3. Using only recently breaking news so it won't become dated by the time it's published

The only way you will get the hang of filler writing is if you plan ahead. Follow the suggested timing in the publication's writer's guidelines, erring on the side of being too early. For example, January is Cervical Cancer Screening

Month, and I once wrote a filler called "What Every Woman Needs to Know About Cervical Cancer." Such a topic must be submitted by June, at the latest, for a January printing. (And, of course, I would always research the latest news on cervical cancer, not simply reuse old material.)

Submit shorts with a cover letter and then move on. Polish your filler until it is spit-shined. Cut all extraneous words. You can simply send your filler to the appropriate editor with a short cover letter, unless specified otherwise. After you have sent out a bunch of fillers, you'll probably have the research-writing rhythm down pat and be ready to move on to query writing. Follow up on your filler submissions after a month, but otherwise forget about them and move on to your next submission.

Spin fillers into features (and vice-versa). Later on, when you are a hotshot feature writer, you can always fall back on filler-writing when you need a break from longer, more energy-consuming projects. And you can "lift" segments from your longer pieces to rewrite and resell as shorts. Some writers even recycle their query letters into fillers by condensing the "kernel" of the idea into a short piece. But be forewarned: One day an editor may ask you to cut a feature-length idea down to filler size. That's bad news for an experienced writer (who gets paid by the word), but for an inexperienced writer, getting in the habit of submitting fillers is a great way to gain an editor's confidence. If an editor has extended the invitation, work with her on shorter pieces until she feels comfortable giving you longer assignments. You'll be amazed how much easier it is to write features down the road, using skills you learned from writing short and sweet.

Crank Up the Filler Factory

By now you know this drill. Run a search at WritersMarket.com on fillers and you'll come up with over 150 consumer markets and nearly fifty trade markets seeking fillers from freelancers. At Funds for Writers (www.fundsforwriters.com), you can purchase an e-book by C. Hope Clark with 140 paying markets for fillers, which is updated regularly. Scan either of these market guides for connections with any of your four audiences first. Once you've winnowed it down, study recent issues of those publications, as well as last year's issues from the same month that you're targeting for next year. Then call the publication to get the name of the editor who handles fillers. After you write your filler, submit one or several at a time with a short cover letter. Keep your cover letter short and to the point. Highlight why you think the timing is right and how readers will benefit from your filler. Don't forget a short bio here as well. Go, mama, go!

Streamline Household Management

The more seriously you treat your writing career, the messier your home may become. I'm not saying it *will*. I'm just saying it *might*. And if it does, the more raised eyebrows you may encounter from your Martha Stewart-like friends and family members.

Get used to it. As you spend more time writing, you will feel the squeeze in household chores and family responsibilities. If the adjustment period gets a little messy, don't panic. You'll get the hang of rebalancing as you go along. Besides, having less time helps you prioritize what absolutely needs to get done and what isn't truly necessary. Here are some suggestions for preventing total chaos in the interim:

COMMAND CENTRAL

Do you have one spot in the house where you collect all the paper scraps of information that come and go in your life? If not, consider setting up Command Central and teaching everyone in your family to use it. Start with a big bulletin board. Add a large calendar with enough space for everyone's activities, and use color-coding for each family member. Next install a wall pocket or cubby for each member of the family. When they receive mail or you sign a permission slip, you know where to put it so they can find it. Tack up some pens to the wall, tied on the end of a string or ribbon. Attach a container of tacks right to the board. Now you have a family communication system. A monthly family meeting can help further coordinate everyone's schedule.

DAILY RHYTHMS

Twenty minutes after each meal is enough time, if everyone is working together, to make the place spic-and-span. Make it a household rule that everyone pitches in during these times, and you will keep a lid on disorder. If that's not enough time, try adding twenty minutes before bedtime to the routine. And before you try to do it all yourself, repeat after me: *No slackers allowed.*

Divide your weekly and monthly chores so a little bit can be done on a daily basis, instead of saving it all up for one massive undertaking. Give everyone a daily chore that can be rotated on a monthly basis. For example, one child could be responsible for taking out the trash and the other for recycling. As for the little ones, they can "play" chores while everyone else gets them done. Depending on their age, a pile of unsorted socks, some pots and pans, or a feather duster is fun to play with! They'll be entertained, and you'll have a few free minutes to scoot around and get your house (and your mind) in order.

BREAK LONGER CHORES INTO CHUNKS

Chores that require more time and effort, like cleaning the bathroom or cleaning out the garage or closet, can also be streamlined. Even if you are used to cleaning in one fell swoop, break larger tasks into chunks and tackle one chunk each day during one of your regular cleaning spurts. If you have more to clean than you can get done in several chunks of time, hire help. Younger teens like money and are often willing to work for it, so hire them on the weekends to get the big jobs done.

For weekly errands, try aligning each task to a day of the week, then do it when you're normally out and about. Post a reminder on your front door until you get in the habit, like "return library books on Mondays, go to the post office on Tuesday, grocery shop on Wednesdays." When these tasks become habit, you will be amazed how effortlessly you keep can keep up on tasks that tend to pile up.

RECONSIDER GENDER ROLES

Do gender roles get assigned at birth, or are they negotiated day by day? They are negotiated day by day, at least in our house. Therefore, even if you have always made dinner and had it ready when your significant other returns home from work, that doesn't mean the world will stop spinning if you decide that some things need to change. If you think certain tasks are your job, or "women's work," or even if you are trying to keep up with your mom's standards of household order, you may want to revisit your notions to see if they could benefit from more flexibility, now that you are writing.

If a mama isn't happy with the division of labor under her roof, it's up to her to speak up and get the dialogue going about alternatives. A good time to begin an ongoing discussion is *before* you become stressed with deadline pressures. Of course, I'm not saying any of this is a requirement for writing. It isn't. But if you feel frustrated or overly stressed, you might want to get the conversation rolling and start troubleshooting with your spouse. It certainly can't hurt.

10

Show Readers How It's Done

After more than decade of balancing a day job as a nurse and a part-time writing career, I began writing full-time one year ago. I'm certainly not an overnight success, but work has been growing steadily. As a nurse, my skills improved with each challenge and achievement over a period of more than twenty years. Writing is no different.

~ LORI RUSSELL, MOTHER OF TWO

D o you know how to prepare an exquisite turkey dinner on a shoe-string? Execute a perfect rugby tackle? Pay rock-bottom rates for accommodations in exotic destinations all over the world? What do you know how to do? Editors would like to know.

If you've ever jotted down a recipe or shared DIY (do it yourself) instructions with a friend, you already understand the basic structure of how-to writing. How-tos and list articles are similar in that they both inform the reader (sections of a list article may even contain how-to elements) and can often be submitted with a simple cover letter (as covered in chapter six). They differ, however, in that a how-to is written as a sequence—first you do this, and then you do this, and finally you do this—whereas a list article does not necessarily contain a step-by-step process.

The essential question the writer asks herself when writing a how-to is "What happens next?" If you are about to embark on a how-to, start at what you consider the beginning, and just keep answering that question over and over again. Before you know it, you will have sketched out a draft of a how-to article.

How to Write How-To Articles

1. Choose a topic that interests you enough to focus on it for at least a week or two. Sit down and write a rough, rough draft. Include everything you can think of. Stay loose, don't get analytical, and enjoy the process of sharing what you know. When you are done, you will have the bare bones of an article that only you could write. Then put it away for a while.

2. When you come back to it, switch gears and imagine you are the reader of this article. Pick three words to describe the audience you want to address (e.g., professional, single, men). As this reader, what questions would you

Don't Forget to Use Your Voice

No two how-tos will ever sound the same. That's because writing a how-to affords you the opportunity to show how something is done, the way only you can describe it: This is called using your voice. Your voice is what sets your writing apart from mine or anyone else's. Obviously, in some kinds of writing you want to tone your voice down, like in informative pieces or news reporting. But in other types of writing, like personal essays, you want to crank up your voice. Regardless of what the final draft is going to look like, you can—and always should—use your voice in your early drafts. Your voice is what brings life to your writing. Here are some simple ways to recover your voice, when you fear it's nowhere to be found:

- Write from the gut right out of the gate—you can tone it down later.
- Study writers who use a lively voice in their writing and save a copy of their work for future reading.
- Enjoy what you write, no matter what it is, so readers will enjoy it too.
- Remember your audience—don't write in a vacuum.
- Read your drafts out loud—if not to a live audience, then at least to yourself.

like answered? You might not even know the answers yet, but list the questions anyway, and find the answers later.

3. If your topic is broad, narrow it. For example, instead of how to decorate your home, how about how to decorate your home in country style on a shoestring budget? That's more specific, and easier to tackle.

4. Then do some research. Good details to include with your how-to are:

- Statistics *
- Facts *
- Quotes by well-known people/celebrities

- Definitions
- Anecdotes (short, illustrative stories about yourself or someone else)
- Quotes/examples from people like the reader *
- Quotes/examples from experts *
- Quotes from popular books on the subject
- References to other media (film, television, radio)
- Helpful tools, resources or products (if many, consider creating a sidebar)
- References to local venues or events (if for a regional/local publication)

Editors dig these

Collect everything you have gathered and put it in a folder, a notebook, a plastic tub, or whatever you like. Don't forget to keep track of sources in case you are asked by a fact-checker or editor to verify them. (You will be asked someday, so this is a good habit to get into.) You may want to sift through your research at a separate sitting from gathering it. Or just go ahead and sprinkle your research in right when you find it. It's a lot like cooking—play around until you feel you have it "just right."

5. With your ideal audience in mind, write a tighter draft incorporating the new information you've collected. Sometimes what you've learned in the process of your writing may compel you to start over with a completely fresh and sometimes better, tighter,

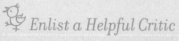

Enlist a Helpful Critic

Who are the best readers for your writing in process? Your spouse? Your mother? Your siblings? Your kids? Maybe, maybe not. Maybe the best readers of your work are other writers, who will be sensitive to the kind of feedback you need. But remember that the only way any reader can give you what you need is if you specifically ask for it. So if you would like big-picture feedback on the overall structure, movement, and rhythm of your piece, be sure to say so. If you prefer that your reader really crank up the critical eye, ask for that. Having the reader ask you questions is always a good idea.

and more focused draft. As you proceed, retain a nice conversational tone by remembering and directly addressing your audience.

6. Next time you read your draft, ask yourself: Is it working? Is it too general, too lightweight, uninteresting, unclear, or choppy? If so, pull out how-to articles you've collected so you can read through them.

7. Be very specific, being sure to include every pertinent step in the process. Remember, how-to articles have to be thorough. You want your reader to walk away knowing exactly how to make that Thanksgiving dinner on a shoestring budget, execute that rugby tackle, or locate great accommodations.

8. Think and write in chunks. If your how-to goes on and on, or off in too many directions, break it down into key points indicated with subheads. Synthesizing complicated information and breaking it down into steps is especially crucial for online writing, and is also a trend in print, even in books.

9. Read the draft of your how-to article out loud to a supportive friend, then ask her a series of questions: Does she now understand the process? Are there any steps missing? Is there anything else she would like to know about the subject? Could she do the task herself? With your friend's suggestions in mind, use your best judgment in deciding what changes, if any, need to be made.

10. Rewrite, read aloud, rewrite, read aloud, rewrite, find a proofreader, and, only when you're satisfied, submit your article to an appropriate publication with a short cover letter. Here's a quick checklist to catch errors or omissions:

- Did you adequately describe the ingredients/supplies needed in order for the reader to complete the task?
- Did you include all the important steps?

- Is the order logical?
- Did you use words that indicate sequence: *first, next, then,*?
- Did you warn readers of possible pitfalls?

If you can check these things off, you have an effective how-to article.

exercise

Hunt for How-To Opportunities

Number from one to fifty in your journal and see if you can come up with as many things you already know how to do. Interested in learning some new things? This is another great source of ideas for your idea bank. Number one to ten and jot down ten things you'd like to learn how to do in the next year. Now think of your parents and grandparents and ancestors. What do they (or did they) know how to do? Make a list of ten. And finally, what ten things will you be certain to teach your children by the time they are adults? How-to possibilities are everywhere.

Luckily, WritersMarket.com has "how-to" as a category. Take a look and run these publications through the filter of your top four audiences (See chapter two). If you enjoy writing how-to articles for consumer publications and you are flexible about which audiences you will write for, you can keep yourself busy for quite some time just writing and submitting how-to articles.

Heroine Worship

Your writing career will not flourish in isolation. Yet too much socializing can be a drain on your time and energy too. What's a writer mama to do when she's getting started and craving connection with like-minded others? Seek out role models for her writing and publishing career. But try not to confuse admiring professional role models with "being a fan." Being a fan is fun, of course, but role models are for studying—whether in person or from afar. Here are four ways you can learn from other writers' hard-won experience and possibly connect with them too.

EXERCISE ONE: ROLE MODEL GROWTH PLAN

Locate the professional Web sites of several writers you admire. For this exercise, your writers will probably have to be either authors or successful freelancers who have invested time and energy in a site. A great place to get started, if you're not sure where to begin, is the Freelance Marketplace at MediaBistro.com. Visit www.mediabistro.com/fm and register to peruse the forum with hundreds of freelancers around the world.

After twenty minutes (otherwise you'll be online forever), narrow your most-admired list to three and research them in more depth. Your goal is to find out as much as you can about the who, what, when, where, why, and how of each writer's career. Start with their site, but use additional materials, like books, interviews, and articles if possible. Start a Professional Development container in which you can stash notes on the careers you are studying, specifically the elements that appeal to you. Take notes on or respond to what you learn in your journal.

Before you move on, make a quick list of what you might see on a future site of your own. What will you be doing one year from today? How will you be spending your writing time? What steps will you need to take to get there? Sketch out a site design on a piece of paper and hang it up where you can see it.

EXERCISE TWO: AUTHOR APPRECIATION

With so many publications that publish author interviews and profiles, you shouldn't have any trouble finding an excuse to contact one or two of your top writer role models. Writers can always use help promoting their work, and volunteering to interview them—whether by e-mail, phone, or in person—is a generous, not to mention educational, act. Just remember that they will be more likely to say yes if you actually find a publication in which to place the interview before you speak to them. If you can't land an assignment, you can always create your own. In my online zine *Writers on the Rise*, I interview the author of a newly published writing book every month and I can't believe how much I always learn in the process.

If you're planning to interview someone you adore, you might want to first get the gushing out of your system by writing a pretend fan letter you don't intend to send, so you can focus on being professional during the interview. You will make the most of your author appreciation by turning your insights into questions another interviewer might not think of.

EXERCISE THREE: SCAVENGER PHOTO-HUNT

Pick at least six writers or authors you admire and see if you can locate their photographs on the Internet. Just go to Google, type in a name, and click on "Images." A selection of photos will pop up. Copy or drag the best one to your computer desktop. Once you've tracked down your top six, brainstorm three words that describe what you admire most about each writer and type those words under each writer's picture. Finally, add a picture of yourself to the collection and brainstorm three words that describe you as a writer. Add your three words to the page, then print and post it somewhere you will see it often. It doesn't hurt to envision yourself in successful company!

EXERCISE FOUR: WRITER MAMA CIRCLE

Julia Cameron, the author of *The Artist's Way,* said, "Success happens in clusters," and I could not agree more. No doubt you have a library in your town and no doubt they have an extensive selection of how-to books on writing and publishing. Why not start a Writer Mama Circle using a book selected and presented by one member of the circle each time you meet? If the book has exercises (like this one) you can even use some of your meeting time for doing exercises together. The main ingredient of a successful writing and publishing group that I've noticed the opportunity for each member to share something relevant that they either have learned or would like to learn. That's why drawing on books that focus on writing and publishing success is so helpful. Because all that is required to "lead" is the desire to learn. More on this, and lots of great ideas for how to form a Writer Mama Circle in your community, at www. thewritermama.com.

11

Trumpet Your Personal Stories

> *You don't need a list of credentials to sell a personal essay. Editors want real stories from real people.*
>
> ~ WENDY BURT, MOTHER OF ONE

Writing based on your personal experience—also known as the personal essay—comes in three sizes: super-short, short, and long. Believe it or not, personal experience articles can and do pay, especially when you choose a target publication first and then write to suit—just as you would select and study a target market when preparing a filler or article. By starting short and working your way up to longer essays, you can build your personal essay writing skills as you go along. Here's how to get started writing essays that editors find highly publishable—essays that are chock full of universal appeal and have conscientious attention to detail, an engaging tone, and lively topics.

Start With Anecdotes

The brevity of the anecdote makes it a good place to start when selling your personal experiences. What's an anecdote? I like Jane Friedman's definition from the *Beginning Writer's Answer Book*:

> An anecdote is a short narrative slice of life, a description of a particular incident, usually biographical, autobiographical, or stemming from something the author has observed. Anecdotes may employ humor, dialogue, or unexpected endings to share insight or illustrate a point. Successful anecdotes will evoke laughter, surprise, sympathy, or some other emotional reaction on the part of the reader.

An example of a market that pays for anecdotes is *Reader's Digest*, where you can earn between one hundred and three hundred dollars for short, funny anecdotes. This, or any publication that pays for anecdotes, is a good target to use for practice because writing short and sweet is key. Just like tips, you won't always find "anecdotes" specified under the Needs section of WritersMarket.com

If none of the ideas from your idea bank jump out at you as potential essay topics, here are some themes to consider:

Turning points	Self-expression
Recovery from illness and disease	Home
Accidents	School
Emergencies	Vocation
Brushes with crime	Willingness to change
Complaints	Death
Crossroads	Dreams
Small and large miracles	Religion
Encounters with amazing people	Redemption
Relationships with spouses,	Nostalgia/memories
friends, children, parents,	Life lessons
pets, and siblings	Adventures
Being single	Humor
Marriage	Spiritual growth or experience
Parenthood	Your first time doing something
Aging	Your last time doing something

(which is where you find other categories like Nonfiction, Fiction, Poetry, Fillers, Photos, Columns/Departments). And remember to revise, revise, revise because anecdote editors are always inundated with submissions.

Study your sample magazine first and notice how already-published writers have connected their material to the publication's specific audience before submitting your piece. What will you write about? A parent can easily come up with parenting anecdotes, a scrapbook enthusiast can easily come up with scrapbooking anecdotes, and a writer mama can come up with anecdotes about being a mom and a writer, given a little time for reflection.

When it comes to practicing your anecdote writing, don't be afraid to sit down with a blank piece of paper and a pen when you stumble across a call for submissions just ripe for the writing. When it comes to writing anecdotes, like tips, studying published samples is more important than anything else. Keep your stories brief and pertinent and try not to wax sentimental or go off on a tangent. Remember the golden rule from chapter nine, and write your draft only twice as long as the final should be and then pare it down. If you find yourself going on and on, you are no longer writing an anecdote, you are on your way to an essay.

Move Up to Short Essays

WritersMarket.com does not have search criteria that distinguish between long and short essays, so your best bet is to hit the newsstands and peruse publications targeting your chosen audiences (don't forget to look in those you already subscribe to) to determine the best place to submit your short essay. For example, *Family Fun* solicits short essays from readers for a dollar a word. Many magazines, like *Mary Engelbreit's Home Companion*, reserve the last page of the magazine for personal essays with a nostalgic ring to them. And some newspapers, like *The Christian Science Monitor*, publish essays.

I once wrote a short essay for *WritersWeekly* about how I broke into the nationals with interviewing. A how-I-did-it essay is one kind of short personal experience essay that magazines, newspapers, and online publications like.

Writer mama Tiffany Talbott published a short personal piece in the Weekend section of the *Christian Science Monitor* in a column called "Been There, Done That." Here's her story:

A woman in my critique group who subscribes to *CSM* told me about it, and I read it for three weeks to understand the tone of the story they look for. It's basically a short summary of where you went on vacation and you answer questions such as: Where did you go? What did you do? Where did you stay? What did you eat? Some columns had the question, Other thoughts?

I submitted my piece on Thursday night and heard back Monday morning. In the first e-mail, the editor said they were backlogged and my piece would run in a few weeks. He also sent a copyright agreement to sign and fax back. Thirty minutes later he wrote and said, "Forget what I said earlier, we want to run your piece this week—do you have a photo to accompany the article?"

A short personal essay in interview format, "Where 7-year-olds Can Help Wash the Elephants" appeared in *The Christian Science Monitor* on June 6, 2006.

How to Develop Your Long Essay-Writing Skills

Follow these steps and you'll be writing one personal essay after the other in no time:

1. **Learn to read like a writer.** There is a distinction between reading for pleasure and reading as a writer. The first time you read an essay, just enjoy yourself, without getting analytical. When you're done, take out a blank sheet of paper and jot down what you remember without going back and looking at it. This will give you insight into what is skillfully written, because usually what you recall are the best parts.

2. **Analyze the essay as a writer, not a literary critic.** The second time you read an essay, have a pen or highlighter in hand. Read the piece out loud and, as you go along, underline any lines you find compelling. In some ways, this process is more a scientific observation than a consideration of the merit of the writing. You may notice fictional devices being successfully employed:

Summary histories	Personification
Hooks	Dialogue
Sensory images	Metaphors
Scenes: people interacting in a place	Dramatic objects

This list of forms is not exhaustive, but you get the idea that, within one essay, many shorter forms of writing are used. Using traditionally fictional forms in nonfiction writing weaves content together in ways that are more compelling than just telling the story "straight." However, some editors prefer a just-the-facts approach, so always pay attention to editorial preferences before you submit.

3. **Draft your essay.** Author Jenna Glatzer discovered the key to grabbing reader interest when writing personal experience articles: Go straight to the

material that prompts the reader to say, "Really?" Once you've chosen that material, develop it into a nice, long, rambling draft. Often, in essay writing, one idea leads to another, which leads to another, and it's only in the third or fourth draft that the final theme of your essay begins to come into focus. This is only natural, so let yourself write a bit before you narrow yourself down. Once you find your core themes and ideas, allow them to guide you.

Give yourself a couple opportunities to identify sections that are working, drop sections that aren't, tighten it up a bit, and expand here and there, but don't worry about finishing your essay in one sitting. If you have a beginning, middle, and end, that's good enough to start. You can always add details and anecdotes later, after you've let your words cool off.

4. **Refine: your last step.** Generally speaking, don't polish your essay until you have selected a target market. The reason is simple: You can't finalize your essay for a particular publication without considering its audience and typical format. So to increase your odds of acceptance, find your market first and then polish your words to suit. Otherwise, you will find yourself piling up a whole lot of unpublished essays.

How to Find Essay Opportunities

1. Writer's guidelines rarely provide specific advice when it comes to submitting personal essays. So when you see a magazine you would like to write for, purchase it to have a sample essay to study.
2. Compile essay markets as you come across them. Rip sample essays out of the publication along with the masthead, and place them in a file you use to identify, study, and submit personal writing.

3. Once you've located publications with personal essay writing opportunities, analyze the writing, match one of your ideas to suit the audience, and write what feels like a zillion drafts (or at least a whole lot more drafts than you ever imagined) until you get it right.

Target Your Personal Writing, Then Write

Within the best-bet magazines you already collected in chapter two, no doubt you have stumbled across some personal essay opportunities. Rip out the essays as you go and keep them in an "Essay Markets" folder. Then each time you sit down to write personal nonfiction, move one of your essay drafts forward to the next level of completion. You can work on several pieces at one time, if you like, or just one at a time. I like to hang my work in-progress on a "laundry line" that goes across the length of my office and keep drafts I'm working on visible on my desktop until I'm through with them. It's hard to avoid my rewrites when they are literally right in front of my eyes. When you complete an essay, submit it with a cover letter (as discussed in chapter six), put it in your follow-up folder, and move on to your next idea.

exercise

Practicing Good Boundaries

Earlier this week, I touched base with a writer mama friend via e-mail. Did she want to chat sometime during the workweek? I asked.

Her response was a list of tasks and responsibilities as long as a freight train. At the end of her message she asked, "Can we talk on the weekend instead?"

"Sure," I replied. "No worries."

"Oh," she e-mailed back, "someone who *gets* it. Thank you!"

I hope the relief in her message will alert you to a little phenomenon you are bound to encounter in your writing and publishing future, called People Who Don't Get It.

SET LIMITS ON YOUR TIME AND AVAILABILITY

Because of People Who Don't Get It, if you are not good at setting boundaries with adults and children, you're going to need to start practicing. I suggest you start sooner rather than later. If you wait until you have a deadline looming to try to convince family members that your work matters and that you deserve support in getting it done, you will be sorry (and possibly late with your work too). And finally, if *you* are not convinced that your work matters, you are going to need help convincing others. Perhaps talking with a trusted friend or writing buddy can help you see the importance of what you do and that your time is well-spent on your writing career.

ASK FOR HELP WHEN YOU NEED IT

Help might mean asking your spouse to pick up a pizza for dinner, do the grocery shopping, or take the kids out of the house for a couple of hours. It may mean trading babysitting with a mama friend. It may mean calling your editor and saying, "Sorry, could I have a little more time?" As time goes on, you will start to become more productive and less panicky about getting your work done. And if you are a little fretful in the beginning (i.e., so worried about "abandoning" your child that you are not able to focus on your work), don't worry about it. Just do the best you can. You'll get the hang of it eventually.

SHARE A BIT ABOUT WHAT YOU DO

Let's not forget that most people have no idea what it takes to be a mom and a writer. Of course they don't. You choose to combine writing with motherhood, which is your choice to make. Take an extra moment to give them an idea of what your life as a writing mom is really like.

This reminds me of a story another one of my writer mama friends told me. At the park with her two young children, she struck up a conversation with another mom. After some time passed she looked at her watch and said, "Well, we've got to go, I have to get back to work."

"Oh, what do you do?" the park mom inquired politely.

"I'm a freelance writer," said the writer mama.

"What do you have to do," scoffed the mom, "go talk to your *editor?*"

The writer mama smiled and said, "Actually, I do."

Don't lose your sense of humor about these types of situations. Just play it cool and share the wealth. Maybe other moms can benefit from your experience.

FILTERS AND ROUTINES HELP

A filter is a method of channeling your workflow to the appropriate place when it comes in, so you can ignore it until you need it and then find it easily when you are ready for it. Because I balance writing with teaching, editing, and publicizing myself and my services, I rely on filters, or systems to keep my workflow organized. Otherwise, my office, my computer, and my mind would just be a big jumbled mess. (And sometimes, when it rains and pours work, as it often does around here, that's temporarily the case.) The rest of the time, I have filters set up that keep my workflow orderly and accessible. So when it's time to act on a project, I know just where it is and I can grab it and go.

Routines like checking your e-mail only twice daily (if you are capable of that kind of discipline) can be helpful in containing the kinds of tasks that can expand infinitely. Other tasks to be watchful of include: chatting with professional friends, surfing the net, building and maintaining community Web pages, reading every newsletter that comes into your inbox, and just generally getting swept up in time-chomping tasks that are not absolutely essential to writing and submitting your work. You don't have to completely cut out the fun stuff, but do try to contain it for productivity's (and sanity's) sake.

For example, you could filter all of the professional writing newsletters you sub-scribe to into one folder in your inbox. Then skim what's less important once a week, on Friday afternoons during lunchtime or late night. Filters and routines can save you a bundle of time.

12

Become a Serial Specialist

> *When you're just starting out, it's worth considering what subject areas you want to work on the most, and trying to build up your credits in those areas instead of just pulling ideas from all over the map.*
>
> ~ JENNA GLATZER, EXPECTING

At some point in your writing career, the question is bound to arise: Should you specialize or generalize? I have noticed over the years that the differences between the two approaches are not so black and white. Let's examine them.

What's a Specialist?

As a specialist, you concentrate your publishing efforts on filling a specific niche, or you target a particular market, such as pets, health, or obscure holidays. By offering your services to one market over and over, you reduce the amount of preparation and research you need to do with each approach. For example, if you tend to write for home, garden, and décor publications, you must still go through the usual preparation before writing your articles, but by the time you get to the execution stage, you have a distinct advantage: You understand the subtleties of editor preferences in home, garden, and décor publications. You are familiar with the jargon, the typical article formats, and what readers want to know and don't want to know. In this regard, a little specializing can go a long way in saving you time and effort; plus, you may achieve a higher per-word rate and receive repeat assignments.

What's a Generalist?

If you are a generalist, you pride yourself on the ability to write in a lively, engaging manner about any topic, for various audiences or a general audience. You will write for any market—women's or men's, home or travel, science or romance—but mostly for those that pay well or have assignments available when you need them. Editors appreciate your flexibility and, often, your ability to produce the type of ar-

The New PMS—Professional Mission Statement

Whether you aspire to work with the editor of a local publication or the executive editor of a national consumer magazine, the drill is the same: When you focus on the positive attributes you bring to the editorial table, you will steer clear of anxiety and awkwardness and present yourself as the professional you are. With your future editors' needs in mind, create your own Professional Mission Statement and post it where you will see it while you work. Your PMS will separate you from the crowd of wannabes and put you in a class of attractive candidates for recurring assignments.

I will strive to bring the following to every editor to whom I pitch or submit my work:

- my highest quality writing skills
- my positive attitude
- my willingness to move a project forward in a win-win way
- my fresh ideas and creative approach
- my intelligence, research skills, and best contacts
- my professionalism
- my cooperativeness and flexible attitude
- my integrity and desire to do the best job I can

ticle they need on a deadline. I once even encountered a generalist who never wrote for the same editor or publication twice. And yet she published national articles consistently. The drawbacks of being a generalist echo the advantages of specializing, only in reverse: You spend more time on research before writing and more time gaining familiarity with language, tone, and audience—and not necessarily for more money. However, flexibility cuts down on the dreaded lag time between assignments and keeps you busy. But before you become a good generalist you need to establish a track record as a writer who can translate any topic into readable prose.

- Electronic Address Book: I manage all of my professional contacts in my electronic Rolodex, using my desktop rolodex with paper cards for personal contacts or only to jot someone's information down until I can transfer it into my computer.
- Two E-mail Accounts: Wendy Burt uses two e-mail accounts, one for work and close family/friends, and the other for newsletters and other subscription-based resources.
- All the Necessities Within Reach: C. Hope Clark says, "I hate being in the midst of creative or business thought and having to get up and search for something."
- Caller I.D.: When she's writing, Wendy Burt says Caller I.D. helps her determine if a call is one that can wait or one that she needs to take.
- Microsoft Office: While it's certainly possible to launch a writing career with nothing more than a pencil and a piece of paper, eventually it makes sense to invest in Microsoft Office, which is the standard word-processing software in the industry. It also has the capacity to organize your e-mail and use spreadsheets to track your submissions.

Specialize Now, Generalize Later

Many successful writer moms specialize and generalize, depending on what's called for under the circumstances. However, at the beginning of your career, you will definitely benefit from considering the strongest cards in your hand and learning how, when, and where to most strategically play them. Kelly James-Enger, author of *Ready, Aim, Specialize!: Create Your Own Writing Specialty and Make More Money*, started her writing career by writing for any type of market she could get her hands on. Over time, however, she realized that focusing on a handful of topics would save time and energy. Based on her past interests, she chose health, fitness, nutrition, and relationships and began specializing. She quickly noticed a major increase in her income; even magazines she was already writing for increased her per-word rate. Kelly's book details the following specialties:

Health

Diet, Nutrition, and Food

Business and Finance

Technology

Parenting

Travel

Fitness and Sports

Essays and Personal Pieces

Home and Garden

Profiles and True-Life Features

As you can see, these specialties are mostly topics. Essays and Personal Pieces and Profiles and True-Life Features, on the other hand, are on this list because they are forms of writing that appear in most publications. So if you have a knack for essays or profiles, you could keep busy by writing those forms repeatedly for a variety of target markets.

Most writers work in several specialties at one time, jumping from specialty to specialty regularly, or they develop one specialty after another, becoming serial specialists. Authors of nonfiction books often hook article writing to the caboose of their latest books to generate article sales and garner interest for their book. And freelancers may work in spurts for certain editors, on certain topics, or for certain types of articles. For example, if an editor likes your profiles, she may send you regular assignments or contact you to see if you have any more articles. So when it comes to specializing, stay loose, experiment, and see how it goes. Don't be afraid to choose a specialty you think you can get plenty of wear out of. But if you or your specialty get tired, feel free to walk away for a while and work on something different. Here are several paths that can help you recognize a specialty you may not even know you have:

1. Background. Your professional background, education, or training are good indicators of a future specialty, assuming the topic is one you are interested in exploring further. For example, I have a M.F.A. in writing, so I often draw on what I practiced in graduate school and have learned since then in my writing and teaching.

2. Challenges. I know three authors who have turned health problems, such as panic disorder or bipolar disorder, into columns, articles, and book deals. Insights gained from your life challenges can benefit others and provide you with a great place to start writing. (Note: Writers without medical credentials should conduct extensive interviews or co-author with medical professionals.) And health challenges are certainly not the only obstacles folks have. My students have written about getting out of debt, getting dogs with muddy paws to clean their own feet, even how to motivate friends and family to respond with more sensitivity to families who have just brought home a newborn baby.

3. Preferred Writing Form. Your strongest and most satisfying skill set can be used repeatedly on a variety of topics and audiences. For example, I've found that I prefer the more interview-intensive process of profile writing to the more research-intensive process of general feature writ-

ing, so the bulk of my assignments are profiles. While the writing-skill set in which you specialize will need to match an editor's needs, there's a lot of leeway here.

4. Hobbies. Topics that strongly capture your interest or imagination are good choices for a specialty. My decorating skills are beginner level at best, but I love writing for home décor magazines and interviewing skillful decorators. (As a bonus, my surroundings usually benefit from a little surge of inspiration afterwards!) Remember: Your personal interests are the springboard, not the destination. Even if you have a certain amount of expertise, you might want to start by focusing on another enthusiast and write a profile—your own knowledge and personal experience will shine through.

5. Interests. What topic do you never tire of? Ask yourself what fascinates you and see if you can make a connection through writing. You might find two complementary paths that feed each other and help distinguish you from the crowd. For example, Bev Walton-Porter combined her two interests in writing and astrology and wrote *Sun Signs for Writers.* What would two or more of your interests add up to? I bet there's some good material to be found in the joining.

Strike a balance, as much as possible, between personal satisfaction and your specialties. What would you enjoy doing anyway, even if you weren't getting paid? Somewhere in the answer to that question is probably something you are a natural at.

Think of the first year of your writing career as a grand experiment: Try some different possibilities before you narrow down your options. If a project grabs your attention or you think you might gain good, solid professional experience, jump on it! If you try one specialty—say parenting articles—only to discover you don't enjoy writing them, you can always reassess and try again. That's the beauty of a freelance writing career. You always have options, and you control the direction, so choose!

Five Ways You Can Specialize

Use the list below to brainstorm the intersection between your most satisfying specialties and the current publishing marketplace. Opportunities might appear on the horizon sooner than you expect, so try to keep an open mind. List your top three possibilities for each specialty idea. Then circle the one you think has the most potential in today's marketplace. Those are the specialties to consider next.

1. Expertise You Already Have: Professional Background, Education, and Training

2. Personal Experience: Life Challenges You Have Faced

3. Preferred Writing Form

4. Hobbies: Topics That Strongly Capture Your Interest or Imagination

5. Your Tireless Topic: The Topic You Are Always Writing or Talking About

The Possibility of Childcare

To use childcare or not to use childcare: That is definitely a good question! Chances are good, when you get to a certain point in your writing career, you'll be ready to consider childcare options so you can expand your hours or work more efficiently.

For some moms, however, the mere mention of the word "childcare" can be disconcerting. I felt that way for the first couple years of motherhood. But in retrospect, I was using some forms of childcare right from the early days: I just didn't call it that. By the time I was ready for more formal childcare, I had enough regular work to justify the cost, and both my daughter and I were ready.

It's easy to feel overwhelmed at the prospect of finding high-quality childcare. But the payoff in peace of mind is worth the effort it takes to choose the routine that works for you and your family. Just remember, you have plenty of options, and you never have to settle for anything less than satisfactory for you and your kids. Here are a few things to consider as you progress in your writing career:

YOUR OPTIONS ARE MANY

The beauty of childcare is that it can be customized to suit your needs. Consider which of these choices might work best for you, if and when you are ready:

- local senior citizen or student (high school or college) who comes to your home
- friend who is willing to trade babysitting time or take payment
- grandparents or other relatives

- a nanny or au pair (daytime or live-in, or share a nanny with another family)
- institutional daycare (e.g., YMCA, church, or corporate)
- licensed home childcare
- preschool (often held at a public school, private school, or church, two or three mornings a week)

When Diana Burrell's son was almost three, she found her writing plate full with contracted projects, so she and her husband hired an au pair from Germany. The summer before, she had had a babysitter come into her home for fifteen to twenty hours a week. Other writing moms echoed Burrell's pattern of starting with in-home childcare when their babies were small, increasing hours as needed, and then pursuing other options once babies became toddlers.

COMPARE AND CONTRAST PROVIDERS BEFORE YOU'RE READY

Research and compare available childcare options *before* you need them. Check local newspaper ads, call friends, and check library or church bulletin boards for possibilities. Most daycare centers have rhythms and rules children must adapt to, so find out what those are and make sure they work for you—at least in theory—before you make a commitment. You can search the Internet for childcare provider interview checklists, then whip up a customized list of questions according to your needs. Down the road, if you do decide to use childcare, you'll feel better because you've done your homework.

THE ONLY SURE THING IS CHANGE

Writing professionally has a lot of starts and stops, especially in the beginning. So it's especially nice to find a childcare provider who can roll with your flow. I change Samantha's hours at childcare almost as often as I reload my printer paper, and I'm fortunate to have found a woman with twenty years' experience who runs a tight ship, lets the kids be kids, and doesn't care what time I drop Samantha off and pick her up.

Try to find a provider who will let you start with the hours that are financially manageable for you in the short run and who will allow you to expand your hours as your workload and income grow. If you are a writing mom, investing in high-quality childcare is probably the largest and most important reinvestment in your business. If you know your children are well cared for, you will be productive and happy and make more money.

CHOOSING NOT TO USE CHILDCARE

When her two children were young, writer mama Sharon Cindrich says dealing with a childcare provider was more trouble than it was worth. So she went back to writing in the nooks and crannies until her kids were old enough that they didn't need her constant attention. Of course, if you want to wait until your child is older to use childcare, or if you choose not to use childcare at all, there are plenty of alternatives, such as trading off time with your spouse, friends, and other family members so you'll have more time to write. And you can probably write plenty of tips, list articles, how-to articles, and fillers with the time you can scrape together.

HOW TO WORK WITH KIDS UNDERFOOT

If you decide not to use childcare, here are some ideas for squeezing more writing time into your busy day without anybody missing a beat:

Take a ride. Strap your kids into a stroller or car seat and take a walk or a drive. Make sure you bring your journal and a pen along—they might be entertained enough by the change of scenery for you to grab a few minutes to jot down a few thoughts on a notecard. And you never know—they might even fall asleep and then you can park and write!

Milk a library visit. If your kids like to read, go to story time, or play with library-provided toys, you can often squeeze a lot of words out of even a short visit. Sit nearby or let them play right at your feet and see what you can accomplish. Better yet, make library visits a regular part of your routine, and the kids will get used to having "quiet time" while mommy gets some "writing time."

Visit kiddie coffee shops. Take your little ones to a child-friendly coffee shop, if you have one nearby. But it works best if your kids are old enough to entertain themselves and get along well with other children. Otherwise, you may not get any writing done, but at least everyone will have a good time. And while you're there, poll some other parents on ideas you've been cultivating. The local joint with the basket of kids' toys can provide entertainment for your kids even if no one else is around.

Make it a regular playdate. Have a regular writing/play date with another writer mama or invite several as part of a Writer Mama Circle. You can hire a college or high-school student to watch the kids in one room while you all write in another, or see what you can do sitting right there on the floor in the same room alongside the kids. As a last resort, one mom could watch the kids while the other writes from a quieter distance, and then switch places.

Go duo. Work on assignments together. A friend and I got a bite from an editor at a national parenting publication by working in tandem on our queries. Consider whether working with a writing/marketing buddy would forward both your causes. Take turns targeting and pitching while the other mama plays the role of test reader, proofreader, and deadline keeper.

Just like Mommy. Set up a table and chair in your office area so your little ones can "work just like Mommy." This works best if you are just doing busy work or don't need 100 percent focus on what you're doing: answering e-mail, updating your Rolodex, or tidying and filing.

III.
Professionalism

13

Prewrite Your Feature

Now that my son is going on four, he's in preschool from nine till three thirty. I can get a tremendous amount done in those hours. If he's home sick or on a holiday, he's old enough to entertain himself while I get a few things done in my office. (Although I admit on those days I'm far less productive than I am when he's not here!)

~ DIANA BURRELL, MOTHER OF ONE

P rewriting your feature is the best way to find your specific topic. If you've done your market research and identified your target audience, then you are ready to prewrite (if not, revisit chapters two and three). The idea is not to write the final draft of the feature you will eventually submit; it's simply to make enough of a start so you become crystal clear about the angle you are going to offer in your query. You are sharpening your arrow so when it hits the target, it won't just bounce off. Prewriting is the best way to accomplish this.

So now is the time to line up all those crucial pieces you need to write your feature (fresh idea, nationally known experts, everyday folks, a timely news hook, and why you are the best person to write the piece) and narrow your angle so that you can eventually write a query that will be perfectly clear.

Nineteen Ways Into Your Material

Don't overthink your approach when prewriting—just plunge right in. Try not to get self-conscious about your idea. Be an explorer instead. Here are nineteen ways to help you get going that will make your final product more lively than a traditional who, what, when, where, why, how approach.

1. **The off-the-top-of-your-head list.** Number down the side of the page from one to ten. What are the ten steps, details, or crucial elements you want to cover? (This also works well for a Letterman-style Top Ten List when writing a list article.)

2. **The letter to a close friend (you'll never send).** The key here is to make the friend someone to whom you can disclose anything. This breaks down formality and allows the use of a strong voice to lead you deeper into your material. Speaking to a close, personal friend is different from

speaking to a large audience, and that's the point. This is good when you are drafting and want to write from the hip.

3. **The mind-map method.** Write a word in the middle of a blank page and circle it. Then scribble down other words as they come to you and connect the circles as you like. This is good for sorting out jumbled thoughts, making connections, and discovering natural sequences.

4. **Sticky note storyboard mode.** Jot down main ideas on sticky notes and arrange and rearrange them on a clipboard or dry erase board until you find the sequence you are looking for. I like this approach when my topic has so many components that I can't find the throughline of what I'm striving to say.

5. **Spin cycle.** What have you uncovered in your research that puts a new spin on even an old, tried-and-true topic? What aspect of the topic has not been examined? What happens if you zoom in, or zoom out, and look at the bigger picture? Make a rough sketch of your topic on a piece of blank paper.

6. **The fill-in-the-blanks procedure.** Write, "What I really want to say is ___" over and over as you move down a page, filling in words, phrases, or sentences as you go. This will get you right back on track when your writing suddenly comes to a standstill. Raise the stakes by saying, "What I really, *really* want to say is ___."

7. **The let-me-run-this-by-you-real-quick spiel.** This is the oral version of prompt number six because sometimes you just can't find the right words on the page until you have a living creature as your audience. Grab your spouse, your older children, or your pet, sit them down in front of you and say, "So what I'm really trying to say is ___." You will find the appropriate words more quickly, but don't tell the whole story just because you have listeners (you don't want to lose your train of thought). Run back to the computer or notebook, in mid-sentence if necessary, and get it down on the

page. The family will get used to this and other eccentricities of the writer mama.

8. **The housewife act**. This approach works well when the house is a disaster or when you have houseguests on the way. No sooner do you dive in and start tidying and scrubbing when—*whoosh*—a whole plot or outline comes to you intact. Of course, then it's right back to the keys. Sorry, housework.

9. **Find "the juice."** Try to squeeze what's really juicy about your topic into one eye-grabbing headline. This one works best if the story actually is juicy. However, it's also a good way to find the juiciness in a story that, at first glance, may appear tame.

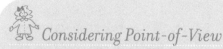

Considering Point-of-View

Sometimes the point of view you choose is dictated by the type of writing you are doing. For example, a newspaper editor will generally expect to see a news feature in third person. A personal essay is most naturally related in first person. And how-tos typically address the reader, often in an informal, friendly style.

Consider what point of view you're going to use in your feature. But drafts needn't be strictly written in any one point of view. Regardless of the point of view you choose for the final version, you can often make the writing meatier by playing with point of view during the writing process. The writing will be richer and more interesting to the reader if you can play with alternating points of view while drafting to find aspects of what you wish to communicate that you might otherwise neglect or forget. So know where you want your point of view to end up and then go ahead and play. Just make sure the end result is a piece that has consistent and engaging point of view.

10. **The inquiring-minds-want-to-know shtick**. What questions would a genuinely curious person ask about your topic? Make that a five-year-old and you'll never run out of ways to approach your topic. List the questions and then get busy answering them. Or pick up the phone and ask someone in your intended audience.

11. **The problem/solution proposal.** Take your topic, break it down into problems and solutions, and propose a way to "do it better." Or list the way a process is typically done and then kick it up a notch to make it a how to do something "best."

12. **The five (or more) senses drill.** Seeing, smelling, hearing, tasting, touching. Come to your senses by considering which ones might come into play before you start writing and you will instinctively find your way in. Pick a sensation, describe it briefly, then see where it takes you.

13. **The opposites attract deal.** Find the natural opposition in your material and play the two off of each other. There's something energizing about opposites. They attract. They repel. They keep any story moving.

14. **The object approach.** Is there an object in your feature that readers need to know about? Then tell them about it. Start with a physical object, such as an apple, a clock, or a toy and tell how it comes into play. Describe what makes it relevant to your angle. For example, in a feature profile, this might be an inherited cuckoo clock that has sentimental value to the subject and your description of it reveals your source's love of family.

15. **The find-the-movement method.** What's "moving" in your story? A speeding car? A rolling ball? A cat darting from the room? Describe the motion. Follow it. Stay with it until it's no longer relevant. You never know where this approach will take you, and that's half the fun. This is a good way to add tension to an otherwise dull topic. (It can kick off an essay too.)

16. **The slideshow technique.** This works well for visual types. Sometimes when I write, a series of images flash through my mind. Start by simply describing what you "see." Then move to the next prominent image, and then the next, and the next.

17. **The set-the-scene scheme.** Just start a scene. To create a scene, put people in place and then shout, "Action!" Your first attempts may come out stiff, stereotypical, or pat. Who cares? Just write your scene fully from top to bottom and side to side. Look around. Don't miss anything. This is a good way to kick off an interview or profile.

18. **The speaker's way.** Imagine you are standing in front of an audience that is very interested in your topic. They are leaning forward, hanging on your every word. What is it exactly that you'd like to say to them? Write it as a speech or presentation.

19. **The pattern approach.** Sometimes we notice patterns or repeated themes in our topic of which we may not have previously been aware. Start with what you initially notice, find a pattern as you write, and keep coming back to it. Some of the ideas you notice that don't fit in your feature might make an interesting sidebar or reslant.

Remember, you're not trying to write the final draft here, just make a start. More than anything else, get the pen moving across the page. You can dive deeper in later drafts.

Rev Up Your Writing

Here is an at-a-glance checklist of ways to keep your writing lively:

- ❏ Write in the present tense (it's easy to slip into past-tense verbs, so go back and double-check).
- ❏ Use punchy, active verbs.
- ❏ Have a clear subject.
- ❏ Keep it moving—say things once and then move on.
- ❏ Imagine every detail as you write.
- ❏ Clarify and be increasingly specific as you polish.

Content Comparison Sheet

Make three columns on a piece of paper and compare and contrast what you've found in already published features in your target market vs. your article idea. Don't imitate the features already published in the magazine, just get a feel for how wide and deep your research will need to be to land an assignment, as you've already learned to pay attention to in section II.

ITEMS TO CONSIDER FOR A FEATURE ARTICLE	NUMBER IN PUBLISHED ARTICLE	NUMBER PLANNED FOR MY ARTICLE
Statistics		
Facts		
Definitions		
Anecdotes		
Quotes—people like the reader		
Quotes—experts/ celebrities		
Quotes from books		
References to other media		
Helpful tools, resources, or products		

Find Your Tribe—Live!

In school, you were probably a member of a team or a club. In a previous job or career, you may have belonged to an association or networking group. And when you found out you were going to become a parent, you might have been invited to join a mom's group. There's a reason for this: There is success in numbers. People gather for all sorts of reasons: to socialize, to learn, to network. And if you want to do any of the above, joining a like-minded group can only help. So, by all means, connect with other mom writers who are just as dedicated to pursuing a writing career as you are.

Connecting in person with other writers whenever you can is important. (If not, "Find Your Tribe—Online!" is in the next chapter.) Try to attend one of the following activities in the next six months. Remember that if you don't put it on your calendar, it won't happen. So schedule ahead.

LOCAL WRITING CLASSES

You can find writing workshops and classes right where you live through the local or regional community college. You may even find them at your local library or community center, so check their Web sites, stop by, or give them a call next time you're in the neighborhood to find out what's coming up. To find a community college near you, visit The American Association of Community Colleges and use their search feature: www.aacc.nche.edu/.

Networking Tip: At the end of a writing workshop or class, ask the instructor to pass around a voluntary class e-mail list as a resource for students who want to stay in touch after class has ended. Ask instructors of e-mail and online classes to share the class list too, if it's not already made available. Don't miss a single opportunity to connect with other writers.

WRITING GROUPS

Want to start a writing group? It's easier than you think. Create a flyer stating what you're hoping to get out of the group. Post your message on bright paper at your local library, your neighborhood bulletin boards, coffee shops, grocery stores, and bookstores. Also contact the closest regional writers association and ask if they will post an announcement to their members for you. You may need to join for that service, which isn't a bad idea. A list of regional writing associations is available at www.writersonthe rise.com to help you get started. Why not join today?

Writing Group Tip: Go beyond the usual critique group format and instead form a publishing or writer's guidelines-swapping group, where the purpose is to help each other set achievable goals and get into print by combining resources and consulting practicing professionals. Writing groups can be a boon to your career so long as members set clear intentions about what they want to get from the group, and then stick to it. Make yours a writer mama circle, if you like. You can always allow non-mamas to participate. For more on how to get started, visit www.thewritermama.com.

AUTHOR READINGS

Unless an author is a household name, chances are good that any book tour is on her own nickel, so why not get out there and offer her your ear? Most authors offer a question-and-answer period after their reading, which can be a good time to ask a career- or industry-related question. If your question is not relevant to a general audience, an opportunity to chat briefly with the author usually presents itself at the book-signing table. This is a great time to offer to conduct an interview for a magazine or solicit some quick advice (as well as get your book signed, of course).

Author Reading Tip: If the author is a writer mama, ask her for an opportunity to connect with local writer moms by having all the writer mamas in the audience raise their hands. It's good networking practice. Or bring your flyers for forming a local writers group and ask if the author will make an announcement about it. In my experience, professional writers are happy to encourage beginning writers.

REGIONAL WRITERS ASSOCIATIONS AND CONFERENCES

If you want to write and publish what you write, no single activity will advance your career and expertise as much as attending a writers conference and participating as fully as you can. Because most writing conferences offer opportunities to interact with editors and agents, conference attendance can be instrumental for advancing your professional skills, learning about a variety of genres, and pitching book concepts. They are also for helping you improve writing and querying skills. Chapter twenty-two, "Count Down Days to a Conference," will help you find and choose a conference when you're ready.

Associations and Conferences Tip: Plan to attend a writing conference several months in advance, as you will want to do some homework in order to get the most out of it. Ask writers you respect who have attended in the past and get their input and recommendations. In addition, you may want to pay for an opportunity to sit down face-to-face with agents and editors and pitch a nonfiction book idea, novel, or memoir, if you have completed one. You can also probably pay for a critique from a professional writer, which can be enormously helpful in strengthening your writing skills. Chapter twenty-three, "Pitch a Nonfiction Book Concept," will help you get ready to pitch at a conference.

INFORMATIONAL INTERVIEWS WITH LOCAL WRITERS

If you have a friend of a friend of a friend who is a writer or who is involved in the publishing industry, arrange a good old-fashioned informational interview with her. Once you've arranged a meeting, think about her professional experience as it relates to your goals and come up with five to eight questions. The biggest stumbling block for most beginning writers is shyness and fear, but remember that this professional was once a beginner, just like you.

Informational Interview Tips: Here are some suggested questions for informational interviews:

- What motivated you to become a writer (or author)?
- How long did it take you to get paid for writing, and how did that affect how you thought about your writing?
- What do you know today that you wish you had known back then?
- What advice or suggestions would you offer a person like me?
- How has being a mother been an advantage/disadvantage to your writing career, and what suggestions do you have for writer mamas?

14

Draft Your Query

> *I got my first three hundred or so published pieces while work-ing at a full-time job. The trick is to structure your time so that the solid hour of uninterrupted time is used for writing (your articles or queries), while the spare ten minutes you can find during TV commercials, right before bed, etc. is used to e-mail editors and track submissions.*
>
> ~ WENDY BURT, MOTHER OF ONE

The query letter is a sales tool writers use to present their ideas to editors. Querying is the fastest and shortest route to making more money as a writer without writing a full-blown article in advance. Writing queries is the next natural step after warming up your writing and marketing skills by selling tips, lists, fillers, how-tos, and essays with cover letters.

But at the same time, query letters are a big step. When you are ready for queries, there is one way to learn how to write them well: practice, practice, practice. Queries are not the kinds of documents you usually nail on the first draft. Don't count how many hours you spend on your initial query attempts. Just go for repetition and improvement each time, because that's what will help you learn and progress. You will become more efficient and profitable with the more queries you send out.

Getting Started

To make the query writing process easier, I break it down into three logical phases to provide structure and order to what can otherwise be an overwhelming process. The steps are: preparation, process, and execution. Though the words themselves may conjure memories of boring college research papers, the query writing process can be as creative and expansive as you make it, so long as the final letter communicates concisely and clearly how your idea fulfills editorial needs.

Step One: Gather Preliminary Info (Preparation)

What will you need in the preparation stage to pull your query together? Here's a hypothetical list of information that could conceivably end up in one two-thousand-word feature:

- One startling statistic to grab reader attention
- Three nationally known expert quotes
- Four to eight everyday folks with something interesting to share on this topic
- Three examples of your own experience, blended into the background
- Two sidebar topic ideas
- One resource list

It would be difficult to offer an article to an editor without first actually acquiring the key information you need to do the writing. Without it, your query (and eventual article) would be too thin. For example, if one writer says, "I am going to interview Dr. Joseph, a leading expert on [the topic I am proposing]," and another writer actually includes a compelling quote from Dr. Samuelson at a leading medical institution or school in the query letter, which writer is more likely to get the assignment? The second writer, of course, because she has already done the legwork and has demonstrated that she knows how to use it.

The less experience you have as a journalist, the more important it is to demonstrate your competence as a writer. Don't tell editors what you *will* do in your queries, unless you have a long list of impressive clips that demonstrate your track record as a freelance professional. Don't give them a bullet-point list of all the material you are *going to* gather. Take your bullet-point list and gather what you need right from the beginning of the query-writing process. That's a solid step toward preparing yourself to discuss intelligently a feature idea, if and when an editor expresses interest.

Step Two: Let It Simmer (Process)

You must synthesize a lot of complex information in order to pitch your idea clearly and succinctly. So don't be afraid to spend some time with your material, mulling

🐑 What Is Plagiarism?

If you haven't run your research through your own thought-process and translated it into your own words, be careful. You may be on the verge of plagiarism: the process of, knowingly or unknowingly, taking another person's words or ideas and passing them off as your own without giving appropriate credit. General ideas are free and can never be owned by any person, whereas words on a page, in a certain order, are copyrighted. In fact, your words are considered copyrighted the very moment you commit them to paper.

The best way to handle this tricky topic is to always be respectful of other people's words. But don't be afraid to take an idea and put your own particular spin on it. Without your unique viewpoint, you're just regurgitating ideas anyway, and that's not going to garner an editor's attention. What's your fresh take on a topic? That's your ticket to success. Just make sure your word choices are original without exception and you are set to write on any topic.

it over, eventually, gaining a deeper understanding of your topic. Most likely, you will want to spend some time free-writing or journaling or pre-planning your feature, whatever works for you. (I discuss that in chapter thirteen, "Prewrite Your Feature.")

Just be forewarned—shift happens. This stage is like an alchemical process where you transform your base idea into something more pure. You begin with one idea, which gets you going in a direction, but after you pursue that line of thinking more deeply, lo and behold, what happens? You learn things you didn't know, have epiphanies, and start making discoveries that lead you in new directions. This is good news, but sometimes, especially when you want to get your query done and out the door, you may feel grumpy. When the clouds part and you achieve clarity about the essence of your idea, you will find the thesis for your query. So stay with it!

Step Three: Consider What You Need (Execution)
The point at which your mind is bubbling with query possibilities is a good time to remind yourself that you are not writing a book on this topic (at

least not yet)—you are writing a query that must be very focused. So you need to make specific choices about which key points to include and which not to include. The best way to make those choices is to compare and contrast the material you have accumulated with an existing feature in your publication of choice. This will give you a better idea of the research quotas you need to fulfill in your query. The "Content Comparison Sheet" exercise on page 138 will help you compare the content in your article idea with what's already in print.

Assess Your Best Prospects

Choose target markets that are the best match with your expertise and skills, as discussed in chapters two and three. In addition, whenever possible, choose query markets based on:

A personal introduction. I got my first clip with a personal introduction from a writer-friend who had already placed an article with Editor A. I mentioned my friend's name as a reference in the first line of my cover letter to Editor A, and she gave my piece a quick read and e-mailed that she wanted to purchase it pretty much on the spot. So my first clip was very easy.

If you have a friend with a connection to an editor or publication you'd like to write for, by all means use that connection. Mentioning the name of a writer the editor already works with can make the difference between your idea getting priority consideration or going directly to the slush pile. But that doesn't mean you can cut corners on preparation. You still need to study the publication, come up with good ideas, and put together a solid query or cover letter.

Mini Glossary: Query Terms

AP Style: refers to the *Associated Press Stylebook,* the standard style of journalism

Assignment: an article you write for a publication that an editor has already agreed to publish

Contributor's copies: complimentary copies of the magazine sent to the writer

Hard copy: the printed copy of your electronic manuscript

Invoice: a bill sent to a magazine for your services

Kill fee: the amount paid a writer if an assignment is made, but later cancelled

On-spec or **on speculation:** when an editor reviews your completed manuscript for publication, without a promise to publish it or pay for it

Payment on acceptance: payment for an article when it is submitted and accepted, before it is published

Payment on publication: payment for an article once it is published (as opposed to when it is turned in to the editor initially)

Query: a letter to raise interest in your work; the way to pitch ideas to editors

Reprint: articles that have been previously published in other publications

SASE: self-addressed stamped envelope (should be sent with every query submission)

Slant: rewording and restructuring your approach to the same subject for different audiences/publications

Style: a writer's unique flair, sets one writer apart from another

Unsolicited manuscript: writing that the editor did not specifically ask to see; if a publication does not accept unsolicited work, send a query letter first

Word count: approximate number of words in your article

An even smarter idea is to ask your friend who knows the editor to review your query or cover letter before you submit it. Take advantage of your friend's insights into the editor's particular likes and dislikes. It can't hurt to ask her to make a few suggestions—if she doesn't mind, of course.

Instinct. As a mom, you already know how to make the most of your intuition, so why not put it to maximum use in your writing career? In this case, I am referring specifically to your ability to determine whether your writing strengths are a good match for a particular editor. Analyze a publication like a freelancer and assess either a strong "Yes" or "No" feeling for each of your ideas. For now, approach the publications with which you feel you have the strongest chance for success.

Writing the Query

Gather the Goods

Here's what you need in front of you when you sit down to write your query.

- Copies of the publication you are pitching (preferably a few recent copies and last year's issue in the same month you are pitching)
- Current writer's guidelines and an editorial calendar (see below)
- Lots of blank paper for note-taking, brainstorming, and drafting

A publication's editorial calendar is usually found in their media kit for advertisers. Before you write a query and while you are collecting writer's guidelines, also find or request the upcoming editorial calendar. Generally prepared six to eighteen months in advance as part of the planning for the following year, an editorial calendar might be fairly general: *Family Fun*'s 2006 calendar simply says that March is "Cabin Fever Cures, Readers' Best Vacations" and December/January is "Neighborhood Holiday Traditions." Others are very detailed: *Pizza Today*'s editorial calendar offers a whole paragraph to describe the June 2006 "Trends Issue."

Wooden Horse Database offers editorial calendars (www.woodenhorsepub. com). For example, for *Redbook's* November 2006 issue, WHD lists:

> NOVEMBER—Reasons to be Thankful: "What I'm Thankful For"—Readers Tell You!
>
> Ninth Annual Mothers & Shakers Awards
>
> Live Your Dream—Readers' Dreams Come True
>
> Real-Life Healthy Life Makeover—Testimonials of Healthy Living

Long story short: Studying the editorial calendar won't replace studying the magazine and guidelines. But the more informed you are before you pitch, the better your chances of success and an editorial calendar might give your proposal that extra insight you need to get noticed.

Gather Example Queries

Get your hands on some sample queries, preferably successful ones and preferably written by friends who don't mind sharing. Be sure to keep in mind that not every query you can dig up is going to be the kind you should emulate. It may be difficult to get your hands on the truly stellar queries, as they are valuable commodities for writers. Your assignment is to beg, borrow, and "steal" (make copies from books on query writing) as many sample queries as you can reasonably study. Start a collection of queries and review them as you work on your own.

Most professional writers will not hand over their hard-won efforts to just anyone who sends them an e-mail (but if you have a friend in the biz, it sure doesn't hurt to ask). To get you started, I happen to know that authors Linda Formichelli and Diana Burrell offer a freebie package of twelve queries (written either by one of them or Eric Martin) via autoresponder when you send an e-mail to queries@renegadewriter.com.

With a sample query in front of you, put on your editor's hat and sit down and examine it with a red pen in hand. What's working? Underline it. What's not working? Put a question mark in the margin. Then go to the most recent *Writer's Market* and check out the "Query Writing Clinic" where editors give their opinions of a strong query compared to a weak query. How'd you do? Can you incorporate an editing step like this into your own query-writing process? It may help to get a friend's input as well, after you have a full-length draft.

Find Your Tribe—Online or Via E-Mail!

Three cheers for the Internet! Thanks to the Internet (and the Internet's sidekick, e-mail), writer mamas all over the world are connecting, reconnecting, and boosting each other's careers in good times, bad times, and confused times (and goodness knows we've all had our share). Finding online groups of writer mamas is a great idea if you are just getting started and don't know any moms who write locally. If you live in a rural community, have trouble making time for writing events and classes, or just have precious little time to spend networking with other writers, check out these helpful resources.

ONLINE AND E-MAIL WRITING CLASSES

The beauty of online and e-mail classes is their ability to specifically address whatever areas you need to work on to advance your career. There are classes that focus on craft, genres, and marketing skills. If you want to learn food writing, you can get online and search for "food writing classes," make a preliminary list, do background research on the course and instructor, and make a selection. You put the date on your calendar, pay by check or credit card and voilà!—you're ready for the first day of class to arrive. And if the timing is not right for you, chances are very good that the class runs several times a year. What could be more convenient?

What to consider when selecting online or e-mail classes: Online and e-mail classes are not all created equally, and the cost may or may not reflect that, so be sure to do your homework before you pull out your checkbook or credit card. Here are some questions to ask yourself that will help you identify what matters to you in an online or e-mail class:

1. Does the class offer opportunities to interact with the instructor, other students in the class, or both?
2. Does the class offer opportunities to learn from classmates' progress?
3. Does the class offer individual critique from the instructor, group critique, or both?
4. If critiquing is included, what is the protocol for critiquing, and are you comfortable with it?
5. Is the instructor reputable, with a proven track record in the area of expertise in which he teaches?
6. Is the instructor experienced? How long has he been teaching?
7. Does the instructor have an advanced degree or depth of expertise that lends credibility?
8. What's the refund policy? If I cannot fulfill my commitment to the class due to unforeseen circumstances, what options do I have (if any)?
9. What is expected of me as a participant (time, effort, etc.)?
10. Does this class provide the specific benefits that I am hoping to receive?
11. Is there a "live" component to the class? Do I have to be present in a "live" online classroom at a certain time every week? If so, is this something I can do?

As with a live class, don't miss any networking opportunities. Ask the instructor to make the class list available to all participants before the class is over.

ONLINE WRITING COMMUNITIES AND E-ZINES

Online communities for writer mamas are so diverse and evolving that it's difficult to write about them without the information becoming quickly outdated. So let's hit some quick highlights that will help you explore current options. A complete list of writer mama resources is continually updated at www.thewritermama.com.

Here's a quick sampling of free writer mama online and e-mail communities:

TheWriterMama Blog (www.thewritermama.com): A blog about all things writer–mama related. Includes photographs, interviews with author mamas, inspiration and prompts, publishing tips, advice across the genres, contests, giveaways, and fund-raisers. A classroom study guide and suggestions for forming local writer mama groups is available at the writer mama blog.

Funds for Writers (www.fundsforwriters.com): This e-zine from writer mama C. Hope Clark reveals funding sources for struggling writers with a dream and special-izes in grants and competitions for the serious writer. Hope sets a great example for entrepreneurial or self-publishing writer mamas and, in her "free time," works with Absynthe Muse, an organization that mentors young adult writers.

MomWriters (www.momwriters.com): Got a writing-related question and need it answered today? Chances are good that a compassionate community member of the MomWriters listserv will respond. This online community of professional and aspiring writers offers support and resources for women facing the unique challenges of writ-ing with children underfoot. Nikki Boehm is owner and list moderator.

15

Plan for Query Success

> *You hear over and over, write what you love. That's not always possible. Sometimes you just have to write articles you don't feel passionate about.*
>
> ~ BARBARA DeMARCO-BARRETT, MOTHER OF ONE

H ave you ever heard that if you want to make really chewy chocolate chip cookies, the key is to first whip the butter, and then the butter, sugar, and eggs, until *über* light and fluffy? If you know this trick, you are probably nodding. There are similar tricks of the trade for success-ful queries.

Anatomy of a Strong Query

Now that you are prepared for your query, study the content guide below. Then identify an idea for your target market that you can plug into a rough draft query of your own. This is not meant to be a formula, just a way to jump-start your query writing. Your goal is to eventually get your query whittled down to one to two pages. The shorter and tighter the query, the better, but not at the expense of a fully fleshed-out pitch.

Section 1. The Query Lede: One or Two Short Paragraphs

If a colleague or friend has referred you to this editor, mention it right away. Tell the editor the person's name, your connection to this person, and his or her connection to the editor.

Next is your best lede (lead), which is the first sentence or paragraph of your query (it can sometimes be lifted straight from your feature draft). The lede may summarize the article, set a scene, or establish the mood of the article.

What's the most seductive pitch you can make for why your idea, now? That's you best query lede. In brief, this paragraph should make clear, in de-tail and with voice, how and why your idea is compelling to the editor's read-ership. Don't feel you have to address the editor. Go ahead and speak directly to your target audience, as you might eventually use your query lede for the actual article. Then again, you may not (especially if the assignment is altered)—but don't worry about that. Your best examples for your lede are right in the magazine you are pitching. I bet you can come up with one that's stronger, juicier, and more irresistible for readers.

Section 2. The Query Guts: One to Three Short Paragraphs

This section is where you demonstrate to the editor (who doesn't know you from Eve) that you have what it takes to write in the same style, tone, and voice of the publication. These paragraphs take up a good portion of the query, as this is where you serve up your idea with authority and panache. The key is to include samples as though right from your feature article within the guts of your query. Here is where to turn up the volume on research and interviews to make this section meaty and engaging. Take as much room as you need, and don't skimp. Capture the editor's attention with your energy and style and don't forget to mention why the timing is, or will be, perfect for this article. You may be able to pull some of these "feature samples" out of the practice draft you generate in chapter thirteen, "Prewrite Your Feature."

Section 3. The Pertinent Details That Describe Your Feature: One Short Paragraph

After you have adequately demonstrated your idea, outline the nuts and bolts of the article. This is a direct address to the editor. Talk about the article as if it were finished, even though it isn't. Include projected word length, any additional experts who will be quoted, how many sources you will include, and whether you will include sidebars. Also mention exactly where in the magazine your article will go. Compare or contrast your idea to an article in a recent issue and state why you feel your idea will jazz readers.

Section 4. The All-Persuasive Bio: One or Two Short Paragraphs

In your bio paragraph, include only relevant information that presents you as the best person to write *this* article. Don't include anything extraneous. Mention relevant personal experience, if you haven't already, to boost your expertise. The final result should be pithy, yet persuasive.

If you haven't already mentioned how much you enjoy the magazine, this would be a good time to do so. Be specific. What do you enjoy and why? And at the same time, restate or echo your idea and its relevance to the readership.

Section 5. The Query Close: One or Two Sentences

"Thank you for your time and consideration. I look forward to hearing from you," or something similar, is the close. Put a little personality into it. Can you make it sound the way you actually speak without sounding too casual?

Congratulations! You've just drafted a rough query. Now let's take a look at a couple of queries others have written. The authors of these queries have done multiple revisions. Also notice that these queries do not imitate the content guide to a T, because you don't want to follow any formula, but find your own style. Use the content guide as a place to start and then write the query that feels right for you. (Please note, editors' names and contact info have been changed.)

Sample Query #1

April 4, 2006

Cindy Hudson
123 Main Street
Portland, OR 12345

Ms. Susie Smith
Editor
Edible Portland
123 Food Drive
Portland, OR 97219

Dear Ms. Smith,

I enjoyed chatting with you at the Sneak Peek event for *Edible Portland* last week. Your plans for the magazine sound very exciting, and I can't wait to see the debut issue when it comes out in April.

You mentioned that you would like suggestions for story ideas to help you set an editorial calendar for the year, and I'd like to propose an article that's sure to appeal to Portland wine lovers who also care about sustainable vineyard practices that produce award-winning organic wine.

Sokol Blosser winery was a pioneer in the Oregon wine industry when it planted its first grapes in 1971, and today it maintains its pioneering spirit by being on the front end of a predicted trend toward organic wines. Of Oregon's three hundred wineries, Sokol Blosser is one of a handful to receive full USDA organic certification for its vineyard. Three years of work went into receiving this designation, but the winery's commitment to sustainability doesn't stop there. It has also been certified green by LIVE (Low Input Viticulture and Enology), and Sokol Blosser's underground barrel cellar was built to U.S. Green Building Council standards, earning it the country's first LEED (Leadership in Energy and Environmental Design) certification for a winery.

Sokol Blosser uses biodiesel in farm tractors, recycles anything that can be recycled, and uses unbleached paper products for labels, wine boxes, and gift bags. It does all this while producing award-winning pinot noir wines. Leading this effort is Susan Sokol Blosser, founder and president of the winery where two of her children also work. "Sustainability is the lens through which we look at the entire operation," says Sokol Blosser, who was interested in organic farming long before she discovered the means to produce organic wines.

Sustainability and organic wines are not the only attractions Sokol Blosser has to offer. Visitors to its beautiful tasting room nestled among the Red Hills of Dundee enjoy expansive views and may encounter resident bluebirds that help to control insects in the vineyards. Picnic tables lure many of those visitors to linger under the oak trees, uncork a nice Sokol Blosser pinot noir, and relax over a meal gathered at local produce markets.

Edible Portland targets readers who love good wine and who enjoy traveling to taste it. This 1,000- to 1,200-word article will inform them about a stunning travel destination in Washington county as well as great organic pinot noir wines they can feel good about ordering when dining out.

I've spoken with Susan Sokol Blosser about the article, and she is eager to be interviewed. Others to be interviewed in the article include Greg Higgins of Higgins Restaurant in Portland; Heidi Yorkshire, former wine columnist for *The Oregonian*; and Regina Hauser, director of the Oregon Natural Step Network. Susan Sokol Blosser is a board member of Natural Step, which provides a science-based framework for making sustainable business decisions. The article will also feature information about Susan Sokol Blosser's next pioneering venture, a memoir titled "My Life in the Vineyard" due out this spring from the University of California press.

I am a freelance writer who lives and works in Portland. Articles I have written have appeared in numerous national trade magazines in the financial, paper mill, and sales sectors, as well as Portland's *Daily Journal of Commerce*. May I have this assignment for *Edible Portland*?

Best regards,
Cindy Hudson

August 2, 2005

Christina Katz
4567 Mama Road
Mamaland, OR 98765

Jane Jones
Articles Editor
Parenting
Time, Inc.
530 Fifth Ave., 4th Floor
New York, NY 10036

Dear Ms. Jones:

Parenting, where have you been all my life? Well, maybe not my whole life, but certainly the last four years. I could have used your insight, sense of humor, and especially your attention to the details of parents' lives that are just like mine.

I found you on the shelf at our local library as my daughter, Samantha, made her usual rounds in the children's room. And thank goodness, because there were my thoughts on your pages. Take the May 2005 issue. On page 23, Lisa Nee says, "Your baby is about to spit up and you face him toward you to avoid hitting the new carpet." Yep, I do that too, and our carpet isn't even new.

On page 72, loving your hubby despite socks (or in my husband's case, not just socks, but shirt, pants, shoes, one item per room as he passes through) in the middle of the floor. Been there, still loving him anyway.

I especially couldn't help noticing the article, "Cheap, Fast Fun! Easy Kid Pleasers You'll All Love—Right Outside Your Door" because I had a similar article idea last year while playing hide-and-seek with my family in an outdoor sculpture park on a nearby college campus. It's always a bit of a shock when another writer has executed an idea you thought uniquely yours—and done as great a job as Barbara Rowley has—but sometimes it's a good kick in the pants too.

While I gleaned some great reminders from Rowley, I didn't see all of my original ideas, which prompted me to think you might be interested in a follow-up article for 2006.

"Get Outside Fast—No Matter What the Weather" focuses on mini-excursions that can be found in most cities and towns around the country and will entertain moms as well as little ones for next to no money. The piece includes a sidebar, "Cheap Tricks," offering suggestions for the most inexpensive outdoor toys that add fun to outings and can be purchased with a handful of change from the family coin jar. In my experience, the parent needs a little pick-me-up like this, just as often as the child or children.

At the time my original article idea was conceived, we were living in Bellingham, Washington—a place where the weather is frequently rainy. Out of necessity, I planned our activities according to weather forecasts. I bet I'm not the only mom who compartmentalizes in this way. So I've made sure to include plenty of foul-weather options for late winter and early spring, when outdoor excursions are fewer and further between and the stir-crazy factor is running high. Other sections include: "Partly Sunny," "Hot and Sunny," and "Cool and Breezy."

Here's an excerpt from "Partly Cloudy:"

Have boots, will puddle jump. The rain may have subsided, but the slide at the park is definitely too wet to wipe down. Why not pull on some rubber boots, grab a couple of sticks along the way, and head off in search of the most promising-looking puddles. Promising for what? Puddle jumping of course. As a kid, this was a favorite post-afternoon-thunderstorm activity. I can still remember the delight of the warm water splashing on my legs. But depending on the time of year and where you live, your puddles may be of the more icy variety. No problem. Have boots, will puddle jump. Just make sure everyone wears clothes that can stand a little mud and understands that this is a special, messy-on-purpose kind of occasion.

Send your little ones to college (or high school or elementary school for that matter). Just wait for one of those Cat-in-the-Hat rainy afternoons when there's absolutely nothing to do and nowhere to go. Then grab your umbrellas, don your raincoats and head for the nearest university or college campus. Forget about hushed hallowed halls where you'll have to worry that your kids might be too rowdy; academia outdoors is a great place to roam with plenty of new places to run. When I took my daughter to Western Washington University as a toddler, we always had fun exploring and the students enjoyed the novelty of chatting with a little one. No doubt Samantha's presence triggered fond memories of siblings or cousins from back home. Our favorite haunts were the sculpture gardens in locations throughout the campus, the brick courtyard with a giant circular fountain spraying fifty feet in the air, and the bustling student center. We had no lack of places to explore and plenty of opportunities to get our wiggles out.

So you get a little wet. If you have a jogging stroller with a rain shield you have probably figured out that the greatest cause for pause is realizing that your child will stay dry but you are sure to get wet. Here's another way to look at it—if you wait for perfect weather before you stroll, not only will you miss an opportunity for exercise, your child will become terribly bored by running out of new images for his or her mental picture bank. And, as handy as infant and toddler videos can be, there's just no substitute for the real outside world. So forget about staying dry. If you make your walk a brisk one and wear layers of breathable clothing, you can stay warm enough, get soaked, and feel great by the time your sneakers are too sloshy to continue. And your little one will be stimulated, warm, and dry.

There's no doubt about it, sometimes the greatest adventures aren't those that are farthest away, they are the ones that are the most often overlooked sources of fun and discovery—just beyond your own backyard.

Interested? **"Get Outside Fast—No Matter What the Weather"** focuses on mini-adventures that needn't be planned and can take place any day, any time, at a moment's notice, when the meltdown factor is imminent. It's a 2,000-word feature with one sidebar (or more if you like).

Sincerely,
Christina Katz

Enclosures: clips, bio, S.A.S.E.

Sample Query #3

March 14, 2006
Shari Downhill
89 Nature Way
McCall, ID 65432

Mother Earth News
Attn: Barbara Brown, Editor-in Chief
789 Literary Lane
Topeka, KS 66609

Re: Story Query—"Life after Lice"

Dear Barbara Brown,

There was a time when nothing could make my skin crawl like head lice—literally. The memory can still make my scalp itch and my hands grow clammy. With four children in various schools—including preschool where toddlers romp, roll, and nap side by side—the fact our family eluded an infestation for so long is surprising. When it did happen, I just *knew* the world was watching—life under the magnifying glass, and it wasn't looking pretty.

Dealing with the psychological devastation and expense of a lice infestation is gut-wrenching for parents and their children. Worse, though, is the fact so many parents beat a direct path to the pharmacy for over-the-counter pesticides after finding the creepy crawlies in our own or our darlings' hair.

The promises are as powerful as the chemicals. Leading over-the-counter head lice treatments contain concoctions challenged for their safety, as well as being directly linked to childhood leukemia, cancers, and asthma. Though study results from toxicology researchers such as France's Dr. Florence Menegaux are labeled "weak" by critics, Menegaux and others aren't balking. Their studies suggest chemicals used in head lice shampoos around the world—*lindane, malathion* and *pyrethroid*—are not safe for use on humans, particularly children. More importantly, head lice have grown resistant to these treatments, prompting uninformed parents to repeat treatments, compounding the chemical absorption through their children's skin.

Karen Tilley, of Princeville, Hawaii insists there is a better way. Tilley operates *Uku Busters*, a service aimed at relieving the embarrassment, indignation, and itchiness of her clients (head lice are called *ukus* in Hawaii.) Over the past nine years Tilley has been teaching and advocating an effective, non-chemical approach to getting rid of head lice, and has made her services available for schools and other facilities in need of *uku* eradication and education.

This dedicated *uku* raider makes house calls and school visits on request (for a reasonable charge) and has combed thousands of heads free of lice. In addition, a special advice section on her website (www.ukubusters.com) sheds light on what does and doesn't need to be obsessed over in terms of house cleaning and laundry following a lice infestation.

The upcoming fall "back-to-school" season accounts for the highest number of community lice breakouts in the U.S. each year. An article in the September issue of *Mother Earth News* on non-chemical head lice remedies would benefit *Mother* readers committed to finding healthier ways of living and caring for their families. I am proposing to write a 1,500-word article focused on how to get rid of head lice without using chemicals, and will include ways to guard against future outbreaks. In addition, I will provide a sidebar on suggestions for dealing with the emotionally loaded issues surrounding head lice, including ways to talk with children about lice in a healthy, loving, and gentle way (based on recommendations from a child therapist, pediatrician, and public health nurse). The article will include a human interest section on Karen Tilley, her methods, philosophy, and recommendations. An additional resource sidebar will also be provided with Web sites, articles, and a *dos* and *don'ts* section. High quality digital images are also available in both JPG and RAW formats.

I have a degree in print journalism with a minor in photojournalism and have written professionally for over twenty years. I have worked as a newspaper reporter/photojournalist for fifteen years on general assignment, business, natural resource, and agriculture beats for publications including the *Modesto Bee*, *Medford Mail Tribune*, *Central Idaho Star News*, and *Kern Valley Sun*. I have also written extensively for *Wildland Firefighter Magazine*, and have been published in *Good Fruit Magazine* and in the agricultural industry newspaper *Capitol Press*. My human interest column series—*From the Heart*—was published for two years in the *Star News*, a rural weekly newspaper in McCall, Idaho. My columns and features have received numerous Idaho Press Club Excellence in Journalism awards. I have included two published article clips for your review.

Last—and perhaps most important—I have been a *Mother Earth News* reader (and advocate) for over twenty-five years, and treasure my collection of dog-eared *Mother* back issues.

Would you allow me to write this very important article for *Mother Earth News* readers? Thank you for your consideration. I look forward to discussing this proposed project with you soon.

Sincerely,
Shari Downhill

Enclosures: Clips

Land Assignments in Four Months

When you are ready to start querying, set yourself up with a concrete challenge within a limited time frame:

1. **Query six publications, one at a time.** If you are still unsure about which markets are your best bet, just choose your top four and two others that you think are a good fit. You can't go wrong with a magazine that fits one of the possible specialty ideas that you brainstormed in chapter twelve. Start with your first choice, but eventually pitch six different markets in a row. That may sound daunting, but planning for repetition is the best way to learn. In my class, students write six queries over six weeks and you should see the progress even the experienced students make from their first query to their last. I suggest you challenge yourself to do the same. You won't become an experienced "pitcher" overnight, but if you stick with it, you will get there eventually.

2. **Work toward pitching an idea a week.** Once you've built up enough experience that pitching an idea a week is "no big deal," you will start landing freelance assignments that pay better—in some cases much better—than pieces written in advance and submitted with a cover letter. Paychecks will follow. If you can sustain a consistent rhythm like this, and build good relations with your editors, you will not lack for assignments. Even if you currently have a full- or part-time day job, you can develop the ability to make one pitch a week with practice.

3. **In order to succeed, you have to fail.** I may as well tell you right now, this is a business in which the failures usually outnumber the assignments for most

☼ The Time-Limit Option

Though not all writers would agree with this advice, you do have the option at the end of your query to respectfully say, "If I don't hear from you in thirty days [or whatever length of time the publication says in its writer's guidelines that it needs to consider your manuscript], I will assume you are not interested and I'll submit [name of piece] elsewhere." Many editors today don't respond unless they are interested in your work. As a result, if you are not keeping track of the progress of your submitted pieces, no one else is either. Including a time limit solves the problem of "Does she want it, or doesn't she?" It gets you out of waiting mode and into follow-up mode, while at the same time letting an editor know that they have exclusive consideration of your idea for a reasonable amount of time for both parties. If you haven't heard back in the amount of time they've requested on their guidelines (if no time period is given, thirty days is a good round number), that's your cue to follow up.

Writer mama Sharon Cindrich says, "My favorite phrase, and I use it with new markets as well as those I have a regular relationship with, is some variation of: 'I'd appreciate a quick thumbs up or down on this piece so I may pass it along elsewhere if it does not meet your editorial needs.'"

The important thing to remember when using a time limit: Don't threaten, don't push, and don't cajole. A time limit is not a means of manipulation. It's just a way to let your editor know that you have read the guidelines and you are going to allow her as much time as she says she needs to make a decision. If an editor needs more time when you follow up, she'll let you know. And, of course, if using a time limit doesn't feel appropriate to you, don't feel like you need to use one. It's strictly optional.

writers, and definitely for beginners. And if you aren't getting rejected, then maybe you need to aim a little higher!

The good news is that each failure improves your chances for future success. Think of toddlers when they first start walking: They fall down all the time! But with each attempt, they get a little steadier, a little more confident, and pretty soon they're not just walking—they're running! So don't look at a rejection as a bad thing. It means you are growing and trying new skills. If you hang in there and keep pitching even when you feel you are outside your comfort zone, you will soon understand that there is no such thing as failure; there is only "next."

4. **Pitch your initial six publications, three times each.** Remember the Hope Clark example of submitting each editor three articles with cover letters before moving those editors to the bottom of her priority list? Well, the same method works for your queries. If your query is rejected, return to the same editors two more times each with fresh ideas before you give up on them.

5. **Stay with it.** Don't even think about giving up on a good idea until it has been rejected at least five times by five more editors. Each time you repitch it to another editor, you can make it stronger and more targeted.

6. **Learn and grow as you go.** By the time you have sent out eighteen queries, you will have learned a lot about query writing and be ready to query just about any publication you wish. Your writing skills will get stronger. You marketing skills will improve. And hopefully, by the time you send out eighteen pitches, you'll have some new clips on their way to use with future queries.

Should You Query by E-Mail or Snail Mail?

First and foremost, follow the recommendations in the writer's guidelines. However, when either is an option, I recommend snail mail over e-mail for your query submissions. While I realize that this goes against the popular advice to use e-mail as much as possible, there are a few good reasons for this, from the writer's point of view, when you are getting started:

Formatting Queries (and Cover Letters)

Here are simple guidelines to follow when you want to send a query or cover letter. Once you get the hang of it, formatting your query and cover letters will be a no-brainer. A good book for writing business letters to market your work was recommended for your Wish List in chapter seven, *Formatting & Submitting Your Manuscript, second edition*, by Cynthia Laufenberg and the editors of Writer's Digest Books.

FOR U.S. MAIL LETTERS

- Print on bright white paper or your professional letterhead (nothing cutesy).
- Use a standard font like Times or Arial.
- Use one-inch margins on all sides.
- Single-space line spacing; double-space between paragraphs.
- Left justify without using indentations.
- Return address, phone number, and e-mail at the top of the page, centered, left or right justified.
- Insert full date, left justified, two spaces below your return address—September 24, 2006 not 9.24.06 or 9/24/06.
- Double space and then insert recipient's name and address, including job title and name of publication (in italics), taking care to spell all correctly.
- Double space and then insert greeting—e.g., Dear Mr. or Ms. [Editor].
- Double space and then begin your query or cover letter.
- Cover letters should be one page; query letters between one and two pages.
- Triple-space between "Sincerely" and your name, so there's room for your signature.
- If room, add an enclosures notation—e.g., "Encl. Clips, SASE"—then don't forget the enclosures.
- Whether or not you use reply cards and SASE, be sure to follow up—never assume, even without a reply card or envelope, that no response equals a rejection.

E-MAIL CORRESPONDENCE

- In the subject line identify your communication and name the topic or title—e.g., Query: Get Outside, No Matter What the Weather.
- Use the same business letter format as snail mail but left justify everything, including your name, address, phone number and e-mail address.
- Lead with your return address or close with your return address underneath the signature.
- To direct editors to clips online, include the URL at the end of your e-mail; if your clips are not online, use "clips available upon request" (be sure to mention any relevant publications in your bio).
- Once you have several high-quality clips accessible online, consider investing in a Marketplace Profile at Mediabistro.com—for 175 dollars a year you will know exactly where to send editors and you can list your expertise and specialties in addition to your clips and contact info (when all else fails, copy and paste the text of your relevant clips into the body of your e-mail, below your letter).
- Avoid sending attachments until requested, and use only standard software.

1. **People aren't born professionals.** When you are learning to write queries, spending time with the physical process of putting together a query package (copying your clips, printing out your letter, addressing the envelope) makes the learning process more concrete. It demonstrates to the editor and to yourself that you are professional. Until you have some published features under your belt, making the extra effort is well worth it.

2. **First impressions matter.** If you make a good impression on an editor, you increase your chances of landing an assignment beyond the one you pitched (editors sometimes offer skillful writers assignments they need covered). And that's only going to happen when you make a professional impression.

I'm not just talking about the nationals; the same is true for the editor from your daily newspaper. When he sees that you have taken the time and energy to put together a really nice query package just for him, he will sometimes be more inclined to at least meet with you and discuss the possibility of an assignment.

3. **And finally, let's not forget the editor's point of view.** Editors are increasingly inundated by e-mail, so you may have to send many e-mails before you capture an editor's attention. There is such a thing as good timing from the editor's perspective, as well as the writer's. Attachments can also present problems for editors: They might get caught in her spam filter. A letter will definitely make a better and more lasting impression than an e-mail. Not to mention, what if—oops!—she accidentally (or purposely) hits the delete button. E-mail barrages, problem attachments, and deleted files can all potentially add frustration to the editor's already busy day, and make her feel you're not worth the hassle—which you definitely *don't* want.

When to Send an E-Mail Query

Of course, there are exceptions to every rule. Sometimes it is a better idea to use e-mail, such as:

- You have practiced querying and you "get it"—you can put together a hard-copy query package with confidence and carry that understanding over into your e-mail query package; *and*
- You have high-quality online clips that you can use as samples of your work, or a Web site with posted clips; *and*
- You have enough publication credits with reputable and well-known publications to demonstrate that you are an experienced professional freelancer who can fulfill assignments; *and/or*

- You've been in the game long enough that you may wish to make brief inquiries by e-mail or phone and then follow up with a snail-mail query package. If you are good at short, very timely, or super-specific verbal pitches, this may be a good avenue for you, especially with regional editors who publish reprints (see the glossary in chapter fourteen). Pitching reprints this way can save you time, and might even help you sell multiple reprints in one pitch-swoop.

Checklist: From Start to Query

Querying, especially when you are new to it, is a multistep process. But if you are like most moms, multistepping and multi-tasking are part of your everyday life, so you should be up for the challenge. When you are ready to write multiple queries, the fifteen steps in this checklist will help you recall what it takes to get from start to query (or use it to devise your own list), until it eventually becomes habitual:

1. Choose a target market (get a copy of magazine).
2. Get the guidelines (put in folder).
3. Analyze the market (find features by other freelancers).
4. Brainstorm ideas to pitch (winnow them down to the top three).
5. Identify minimum requirements (editor expectations) by assessing existing article(s).
6. Gather appropriate research, contact experts, conduct interviews, etc.

exercise

7. Freewrite your feature until you know the essence of what it's about.
8. Draft your query (on letterhead or in business format).
9. Let it cool off and rewrite a few times.
10. Pump up your words until your writing is crisp and lively.
11. Ask at least one person to read it and ask you questions.
12. Finalize and proof.
13. Send by snail mail (or e-mail if specified).
14. Make a follow-up note on calendar and choose dates to begin two more queries.
15. Start all over again, only this time, it's a little bit easier!

Keep at it. You will get the hang of this, I promise!

Uncover Your Beliefs About Editors

As a writer you have to learn to serve two masters: your editor and your readers (audience). And because an editor's job depends on the ability to watch the bottom line, work in harmony with the sales side of the business, and get the highest-quality content in front of readers, editors tend to develop an edge that can freak some moms out. As much as you may want your editor to get back to you right away about your submission, give you detailed feedback on the strengths and weaknesses of your piece, and tell you what a talented writer you are, try your best to understand that your editor does not have time, nor is it her job to:

- hold your hand or make your job easier
- praise you and encourage you when the assignment gets grueling
- listen to your personal problems or help you figure out what you need
- remind you, read your mind, or help you reschedule when a deadline is fast approaching
- recognize your unique brilliance and shower you with praise for it

Remember, it's an editor-eat-editor world out there, and if yours has to babysit you, she may as well hand her time card over to the editorial assistant who works under her. And any writer who sees any of this as a shortcoming on the editor's part, a travesty of justice, or the reason the industry is so commercialized is probably wasting an editor's precious time and energy. Bottom line: Working with a time-waster is not sustainable for an editor in today's competitive marketplace, so moms can't afford to be sloppy when it comes to editor interactions.

IT'S NOT QUITE SO BLACK & WHITE

I'm putting the above in straightforward terms in hopes of reminding you that the climate in your home and the climate in a corporation or business office are usually quite different. Before you pick up that phone and dial your editor, you might want to ask someone to watch the kiddos for however long you need, put your household concerns momentarily on hold, and take a moment to gather your thoughts (and yourself, if necessary). Homelife gets hectic, and what is permissible behavior in one home may be quite different from others. Be sure to create a little separation between home and work before venturing into territory in which you are unlikely to find pacifiers, *Sesame Street*, and a menagerie of stuffed animals.

You may think, "Oh, my editor will understand." And you may be right, especially if your editor is a mom. But she—or he—may also be young, single, and have little compassion for moms. (Don't be angry; they will likely find out someday how challenging it is to juggle work and home.) If overly casual behavior becomes the norm, your editor may become concerned about how you present yourself to sources and experts when representing their publication. Bottom line: Communicating with the outside world, whether editor or source, is a professional interaction. Treat it that way and watch your career expand. Shrug it off and risk your opportunity for growth. The best way to handle business communications is to remember that you are a mom *and* a professional.

EDITOR-PHOBIA CURE-ALL: FOCUS ON CLIENT SERVICE

From the nervous jitters when hitting the Send button, all the way to a full-blown anxiety attack whenever you think about speaking to an editor on the phone—or, heaven forbid, in person—chances are good that you fall somewhere on the editor-phobia spectrum. And whether you have a mild case or the chronic, fatal-to-your-writing-career kind, it pays to go straight to the cause of the problem and dig it out before you go any further.

No matter where you enter the playing field (as a freelancer, author, ghostwriter, copywriter, you name it), publishing is a business—your business—and editors are, first and foremost, your clients. Writers provide the service of writing, which results in a product to suit the client's needs. This does not make you a servant, or any less creative or hard-working. It simply makes you a writer attentive to the needs of the person who delivers your carefully crafted words to (sometimes large) audiences, often championing them against the skepticism of salespeople and amidst tumultuous office politics.

BE A PLEASURE TO WORK WITH

Eat your emotional Wheaties, mama. Projecting a whole lot of garbage onto your editor is not going to improve your ability to reach their audience in any way, shape, or form. Recognize your insecurity and self-doubt as the inner oppressors that they are. Then put them—not editors—in their place. And relax! You're a writer, and your job is to write as best you can. If you polish up your customer-service attitude and become a pleasure for editors to work with, you will never be out of work as a writer.

WHAT DOES IT TAKE TO BE AN EDITOR'S DREAM WRITER?

When it comes right down to it, being a responsive writer isn't all that different from being a responsive mom. Here's all you need:

- An awareness of your client's needs
- A genuine desire to fulfill your client's needs
- A cooperative and flexible attitude as you work on projects
- Service skills and friendliness towards others
- Keeping your editor updated on progress and necessary changes
- Your ability to deliver the product you promised
- Accommodating your client's schedule and meeting his or her deadlines, including ongoing sensitivity to your editor's availability

16

Go Get the Interviews

> *You can be interviewing someone with whom you feel you have absolutely nothing in common—a medical doctor, a world traveler, an attorney—and yet, mention children, and there is a universal connection, understanding, and mutual respect that connects all of us parents.*
>
> ~ SHARON CINDRICH, MOTHER OF TWO

I f you are a shy or inexperienced writer mama, the thought of interviewing may trigger the cold sweats. But moms are all about asking questions and lots of them, right? *What did you have for lunch? What time will you be home? Do you feel hot? Will his parents be there? Where's your homework?* And if you start with short interviews, you will surely find that interviewing is a lot easier than you think. You'll also learn that one of the most important lessons of interviewing, whether long or short, is not to overdo what could just as easily be done in brief.

How to Conduct Short Interviews

As you learned in chapter fifteen, the more meaty your query, the better your chance of landing an assignment. So don't hope to get quotes for your feature *after* you get the assignment. Go get the key quotes and put them in your query before you submit it. And when you're ready to gather those key quotes, take a look at these tips. They will save you time and calm your pre-interview jitters.

Whom to Interview

Decide whom you need to interview, why, and what specific information you need. Consider the most appropriate sources for the topic, the market, and the editor's preferences. Take all of this into consideration before selecting your best source.

As always, *don't forget to check published examples in the publication you are pitching.* If you see a nationally or internationally known name in the publication you are pitching, make sure that your experts carry the same *oomph*. Cutting corners in this regard—using a local expert when a nationally known expert is called for—is a sign of laziness.

Where to Find Sources

If you want to decide quickly who is the best person to interview for your piece, just come up with three keywords that describe the kind of source your edi-

Smoke Out Qualified Experts

Authors with recently published books. *Publishers Weekly* and the Publishers Lunch e-mail newsletter are two places to learn what's coming up on the literary horizon. Soon-to-be-released books are often pre-posted on Amazon.com along with published books. Try typing into Google "author" or "expert" with your topic to see what comes up.

University faculty or researchers. Academics often conduct studies, surveys, and reports and publish scholarly texts and papers. If someone is on staff at a major university, you generally won't need to verify their credentials. If you're looking for a media-friendly academic, keep your eyes open while perusing articles in competitive publications in your specialty and make a note in your Rolodex for future reference.

Not-for-profit organizations and professional associations. Looking for a freelance journalist? Contact the American Society of Journalists and Authors. Looking for stats on women's career advancement? Try Catalyst, a nonprofit that specializes in expanding opportunities for women and business. Looking for an M.D.? Try the American Medical Association. Nonprofits and associations always like to see their members in the spotlight, so they will be more than willing to connect you with the qualified experts you seek.

Profnet. The purpose of Profnet is to put journalists in touch with expert sources. Enter as a "journalist," register, and then you can send an inquiry or search the database to access thousands of experts for free. You can also sign up to receive e-mail tipsheets on Profnet experts' timely topics. More at http://profnet3.prnewswire.com.

The Yellow Pages. If all you need is a basic medical quote and not the latest groundbreaking study, try your own M.D. If a local car mechanic will work just as well as a syndicated columnist mechanic, call yours. When you are looking for everyday folks, you can always poll the friends, colleagues, and friends-of-friends who match the specifications you are looking for.

tor prefers (you know from your research). For example, *doctor, research expert, nationally known* all describe a different kind of doctor than *doctor, general practitioner, local*. Next ask yourself where you would find such a doctor and go straight to that source. "Smoke Out Qualified Experts" offers you a list of places to get started.

Phone vs. E-mail vs. In Person

Decide if you need to do the interview in person or by phone or if you can use e-mail. Obviously, e-mail is convenient, but sometimes the nature of your article—for example, if you need spontaneous responses or if you are doing an interview that is investigative or controversial—requires a phone or in-person interview.

Another factor is the "depth" of your story: For a filler, an e-mail interview might be adequate, assuming it works for your source, while for a feature profile, a phone or in-person interview would be more appropriate.

Decide which method is most suitable before you approach your source. And early in your career, it doesn't hurt to err toward the live interview side, just to get the practice. Conducting in-person or phone interviews will expand your interviewing skills in a way e-mail interviews cannot. So if you have your eye on a long-term career, go for live interviews.

How to Request an Interview

Imagine that you are reaching out your hand to meet someone while you introduce yourself. As in, "Hi, I'm Christina Katz. Nice to meet you. I'm preparing to write an article on …" That may sound formal, but this is an interview, so it's appropriate to be formal, no matter how brief your inquiry.

If you are simply collecting a few short quotes, you might try a strategy that Wendy Burt uses. She calls sources after business hours and leaves a quick list of questions on the answering machine or voicemail. She invites an e-mail response, which usually arrives the next day, thereby saving precious daytime work minutes.

If you can find a source's e-mail address and you have plenty of time, chances are good that this is an acceptable way to approach them. However, different people have different sensibilities about technology, so be sensitive to that. If you don't hear back within twenty-four hours or so after an inquiry, pick up the phone and call.

When making initial contact with a source via e-mail, be as straightforward as possible. Here's what a typical short interview request might look like:

Dear Ms. Expert,

My name is Christina Katz and I am writing an article on women making time for themselves. Since you [have recently published a book on this topic, etc], I wonder if you would have time to answer a few questions as part of my research. I hope to quote you directly in the article.

I have placed the article with [*A Very Reputable* magazine]. May I send you three or four questions via e-mail?

Sincerely,
Christina Katz
Freelance Journalist
(my e-mail address, phone number and Web site)

A phone contact would involve a similar introduction to who you are and what you need, only verbal.

How to Prepare for Your Interview

Get to know your source's background before the interview begins and come up with relevant questions. Obviously, the longer the interview, the more time you will spend preparing. For a filler, you need to know just the facts about your source, verify her identity (make sure the person is who she says she is), and move on to preparing your questions. For a feature, conduct more in-depth research, which may involve library or online research, reading books, articles, or blogs, or talking to people who know your source. Somewhere along this spectrum is the right amount of preparation for your interview. As you gain experience, you will learn how to gauge how much is just the right amount. In your early interviews, however, it's not going to hurt to be overprepared. Do your homework and trust your gut.

Note-Taking vs. Recording Devices

Journalists are trained to conduct interviews by taking notes. If you feel comfortable doing this, try to capture as many exact words as you can. If you are not, be sure you have a backup plan. Using a recording device is good if you ever need to provide evidence of a quote that is recanted—but you must always let people know when they are being taped and when they are not being taped. And don't be surprised if they make a remark, then qualify it by saying that they prefer that information or quote not appear in the interview. If that happens, you can always ask for another, more permissible quote.

I still use an old-fashioned answering machine that goes through my phone line and records onto regular-size audiotapes, but you can pick up the latest, greatest recording gizmos at your local electronics store, usually quite inexpensively. When purchasing any kind of technological equipment, I prefer to go to an actual store instead of ordering online, so I can get all my questions answered in advance by a salesperson.

How Familiar to Be During an Interview

You should be friendly and professional, focused but conversational. Don't expect your source to keep an interview on track, or alert you to how much time they have. If you are conducting a longer interview, let your source know in advance how long you estimate the interview will take.

A good rule of thumb is to remember that people are busy and will make room for what you ask for and not more than that. If your source is expecting a short interview but more questions come up in the moment, be courteous and ask if they have time for more questions before charging ahead. Then be sure not to run over that amount of time.

How to Ask Sharp Questions

Be engaged by your topic. Be sure you get your head into it before picking up the phone or sitting down in person for an interview. Some of the best questions will come up naturally as you compile your research and during the interview itself. Once you have about twice as many questions as you need, pare down your list according to which would be of most interest your readers. Choose an order that seems conversational. Be sure to include enough of your source's background information in your questions that you come across as informed and professional.

How to Get the Best Quotes

Even when you're using a tape recorder, it's always a good idea to take notes during the interview by hand. (I always print my questions out triple-spaced so I have plenty of room to jot remarks and reminders during a live interview.) As soon as possible after the interview, take a few minutes to list or circle specific points relevant to your current assignment. If you do this while the material is fresh in your mind, it will be easier later to pull out the key responses you need, without having to transcribe or listen to the entire tape. For feature-length interviews, you will need to transcribe the entire tape yourself or hire a transcriptionist.

What to Do If Your Source Goes On and On—or Worse, Clams Up

If your source runs at the mouth, you want to be friendly, but to the point. Steer the conversation clear of excessive digressions, both yours and the source's. Try not to interrupt, but take advantage of natural pauses to take command of the interview and keep it moving in the direction you'd like it to go.

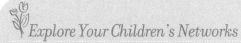

Explore Your Children's Networks

Who do your children know? What do their parents do? How else can your children help you network for interesting sources? For example, if your son makes friends at school with a girl whose father is a pediatric dentist, you might interview him for some tips on helping kids deal with dental-visit jitters. If your child's teacher won the state Teacher of the Year award last year, you can probably pitch a profile or how-to article featuring her tips and tricks for inspiring excellence in her students. Think about the people your children know, and then make a list of parents, teachers, coaches, professionals, specialists—anyone you can think of who might be interesting to contact now or in the future. These are all good places to find interview subjects.

The way to avoid sources who clam up is to let the conversation warm up for a few moments before you plunge in to the interview. Ask him what kind of day he is having, if he's read the latest book on the topic about which you are interviewing him, the weather where he lives … anything! If your source senses that you are relaxed, he will relax. If you are looking for a scoop, try a straightforward but cheerful approach. Most people who tense up feel nervous and self-conscious. They may have been burned in an interview before—misquoted or misrepresented—which makes them mistrustful of journalists in general.

What Sources Expect From You

Sources expect you to be courteous and respectful and to communicate clearly what you need and what they can expect. If you will send a copy of the article, say so (if your editor won't take care of it, ask for an extra copy of the publication so you can send the issue to the source). If not, let them know how they can get it. For short interviews, an e-mail thank you is appropriate; for long interviews, a handwritten note should be sent. Use your judgment. Every time you contact an expert, leave the door open for working with them again in the future.

What-Ifs

What if the source wants to "approve" the article before it goes to your editor? There is really only one scenario in which this is appropriate, and that is if you are not sure you understood the quoted material correctly: a statement was hard to hear on the tape, for example, or easily misunderstood. Either way, if you are unsure, simply call the source and run the quote by them verbally. Give them the context, if necessary. But avoid sending transcribed interviews to sources for "approval." In blunt terms, you didn't ask them to write the interview; you asked them to give you an interview. It's in your capable hands after that.

On the other hand, if you get home, start typing, and realize that you've forgotten something that is a key point, call them up and ask for a few more minutes of their time. For a short request, you might be able to use e-mail. If, as recommended above, you left the door open after the initial interview, your source won't be surprised or perturbed to hear from you. But if he is, emphasize your intention to deliver the best possible interview for readers, and he will appreciate your conscientiousness.

Interview Practice

When I was assigned an interview in a junior high school class, I was so scared that I interviewed my own mother! So don't think I don't know that interviewing can be scary. That's why your assignment is to conduct two interviews. For the first, come up with five questions on a fairly narrow topic and interview a friend or friend of a friend. Tell her it's just for practice, but put yourself through all the steps. I'd be willing to bet that you quickly learn interviewing is fun and want to do it again.

For the second, stretch yourself by lining up an interview outside your comfort zone. If you've never interacted with an author, that's a good goal. If you're nervous about talking to doctors at prestigious universities, try them. Choose an expert whose input you can use on an upcoming query, and make it a short interview, so you'll actually do it. You don't need to have an assignment in hand as long as you let them know what publication you are aiming for. Ready? Prepare! Dial! You can do it! Once you get going you will never look back.

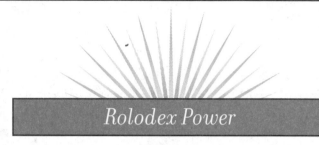

Rolodex Power

Journalists know they are only as good as the breadth and depth of their Rolodex. But from a more poetic point of view, every person is a doorway to a whole new world when you take the time to ask a few thoughtful questions. And sometimes, people you already know—or meet in passing—make fascinating sources for articles, interviews, and profiles that keep the cash rolling in.

POLLING POWER

Early in my career, when I was overwhelmed and didn't know where to start, I took a closer look at four of my college friends and realized that three of them were working moms trying to stay sane as they juggled work and motherhood. I wasn't a mom yet myself, but when I found a Web site purchasing articles on this topic, I started asking my friends some questions. And they told a friend, who told a friend, and next thing you know—thanks to e-mail—I never ran out of story ideas or sources for my eventual thirteen articles on Bluesuitmom.com. When one of my stories was spotted by a producer on *Good Morning America* four years later, my daughter and I were flown to New York to chat on live TV with Diane Sawyer. All because I asked a few good friends some nosy questions!

CONNECT LOCALLY

When we moved to a new town so my husband could take a job at the local high school, I didn't know a soul for hundreds of miles. But after I took a gig writing for *The*

Oregonian, I was isolated no more. In fact, four of the recreation stories I covered introduced me to instructors I liked so much that my daughter has attended their swimming, horseback riding, dance, and soccer activities. You can't beat the combination of a steady paycheck with work that gets you out and about connecting with interesting people you might not otherwise meet.

RESHUFFLE YOUR CARDS

If you haven't done so lately, bring your list of contacts up to date. Go through every entry and jot a few notes about what each person does or what words characterize them (like you did in chapter two for yourself): Mom, Poet, Gardener, Business Owner, Lawyer.

When you are done, sort your contacts into lists by their characteristic words. With an electronic Rolodex you can usually use a sorting feature to group your contacts. With the old-fashioned Rolodex, pull out the associated cards and place them next to each other. How many folks do you have in each category? Notice any patterns among them based on what you know about them? Perhaps two columns emerge, coming from opposite perspectives—for example, organic and non-organic gardeners. That's interesting. Perhaps your poets are openly poets or secret poets. Is there an article idea there? No doubt when you are finished brainstorming, you will have some fresh article ideas and a new appreciation for your friends.

PLEASED TO MEET YOU!

Every time you leave the house, you encounter people who are experts. I discovered this when my husband and I attended a reading at a local Barnes & Noble. Afterwards, I took the opportunity to ask the author if I could interview her. She said yes, and I ended up with a long version of the interview, which I pared down and sent to *Science of Mind*. Because the author was a former United Church of Religious Science minister and *Science of Mind* is their publication, I had a reply from the editor within twenty-four hours. When I mentioned that there was a longer version, he wanted to see it, and I had a contract.

CAN I COME OVER TO YOUR HOUSE?

I had a hunch that the shop owner of my favorite home décor store in Bellingham, Washington probably had an amazing home. One day while she was restocking shelves, I struck up a conversation about the possibility of shooting some photos. As it turns out, I guessed right: Her home is stunning! I submitted my query to Editor One, who passed it on to an editor at a sister publication (which I had actually queried a year earlier, unsuccessfully). But this time, Editor Two gave me an assignment. (Unfortunately, my source sold her retail store before I received the assignment, but Editor Two assigned me another story, so my efforts still paid off in the long run.) After a couple of pitches and rejections, I placed the eight-page home tour.

WRITE ABOUT AUTHORS YOU LIKE TO READ

If you are a writer, chances are good that you are also a reader. And if you'd like to read books pre-publication, you could probably line up some book review gigs with your local paper based on your genre preference. Or you could interview authors who interest you for profiles and features. Because editors constantly need interviews and profiles related to news, this is a great way to crack publications that might otherwise be difficult for you to break into.

Always look for win-win-win situations: Interview people who interest you, hone your interview writing and profiling skills, and break in to better-paying, wider-circulation publications as you become a more skillful interviewer.

17

Negotiate Like a Barter Queen

If you set a figure that's higher than what you've made before, you may think, I can't do this! But you can. Break the number into a daily goal, assuming you'll work 240 days out of the year—that's Monday through Friday, with four weeks off for holidays and vacations.

~ KELLY JAMES-ENGER, MOTHER OF ONE

ongratulations—you have received an offer to write for a publication! This is a happy day! But even though you may be known in your neighborhood for your spirited garage sale negotiations, your willingness to express a contrary view at town meetings, or just for your spunky attitude in general, don't be surprised if, when it comes time to negotiate rights and pay for your writing, you feel flustered and unsure of yourself.

Relax. You negotiate with your kids all the time. And if you're married or partnered, you have had some practice there as well. Single parents and mothers of children with special needs are no strangers to advocating for their children. With a little confidence and knowledge of contract language, you'll be negotiating offers like a pro in no time. So get ready to channel your inner barter queen: You've got deals to make.

What Am I Selling?

When you submit your work to an editor, you are offering rights to use your writing in exchange for money. You have a legal right to control the use and reproduction of your words, but so does anyone who buys them from you (including publishers). Essentially, rights only include what is specified and nothing extra. The only package deal is all rights. They can generally be categorized from highest pay to lowest pay, as follows:

All Rights
All rights are usually purchased by the highest-paying publications (usually over one dollar per word). This means that the publication buys all rights to your article and can use it however it likes: in the first printing, subsequent printings, anthologies, electronic rights, ad infinitum. These rights apply to the words ex-

More Questions About Rights

Do I Need to Copyright My Material?

A registered copyright is not necessary since everything you write is automatically yours from the moment you write it. In fact, when working with editors, the copyright symbol on your manuscript may be considered a sign of inexperience. And don't feel badly if you didn't know this—I did it. Some writers are copyrighting their material these days, but when you are just getting started, you have enough things to worry about. Remember that your words in the order you put them on paper are technically copyrighted as soon as you write them.

Do I Need a Contract?

No. There will seldom be a contract with online publications and small publications. You simply receive an e-mail stating the proposed terms from the editor. Don't be afraid to ask for more information or clarification: Be sure you know exactly what kind of rights the publication is looking for, how much you will be paid, and when you can expect to be paid. This is usually spelled out in the writer's guidelines, but if not, ask up front what terms they use with freelancers. Keep a written record if possible.

How Much Rewriting Is Enough to Qualify as a Rewrite?

If you want to resubmit an article to a different publication, the changes must be significant: a new title, lede, quotes, and conclusion. A better way is to find a new slant or approach and write a new article altogether. Facts are reusable. However, it is not a good idea to write a very similar piece that will appear in direct competition with the magazine you initially wrote for. The solution is to resell to noncompeting markets, which means two totally different types of markets or two publications with non-overlapping territories.

actly as you wrote them, in the order you wrote them—not the idea that you wrote about—but the publication can make editorial changes to what you submitted. You are free to use the same idea in other words elsewhere, but you cannot resell or reuse the original piece, ever. Some publications that claim to want all rights will settle for first rights if you simply ask. You may as well ask because it makes sense to keep as many of the rights to your work as you can.

First Rights

Typically purchased by magazines, newspapers, and online publications, first rights are advantageous to the writer because you can sell the same article, without changing a word, again and again as second or reprint rights. (Reprints only occur after *publication* of the first article, not after *submission* of the first article.) The first print rights known as FNASR (First North American Serial Rights) apply only to North American magazines and do not include anthology rights or electronic rights.

Second or Reprint Rights

The minute a first rights sale goes into print, you can sell the article again, as-is or modified, as second or reprint rights, unless you agreed to an exclusivity period in your contract. Exclusivity means that you've sold the exclusive right to your work either indefinitely or for a limited period of time; non-exclusivity means that even though you've sold some rights, you've retained the rights to republish your work. Be sure you know who's got what before you resell your writing.

When querying or submitting reprints, make sure you include the following information: who bought first rights, when and where the article appeared, and an offer of second or reprint rights. Generally, an editor who purchases reprints will not expect exclusive rights or use of your piece in multiple media, but always read the fine print.

Electronic Rights

Be aware of exactly what you are selling when you are selling to print publications that want electronic rights. Electronic rights can involve first electronic rights, one-time electronic rights, Web publication rights, archival rights, electronic distribution rights, and all electronic rights. Consider whether you want to be paid extra for this.

First electronic rights: The buyer has the first chance to publish your words electronically online, probably in an e-zine or a newsletter. This means others may purchase your piece for republication electronically, as long as it's after the first electronic rights publisher.

One-time electronic rights: The buyer can publish your piece one time only, as opposed to multiple times in a variety of media (e.g., not on multiple Web sites *and* in an e-zine). This means others may purchase your piece for re-publication electronically and publish at the same time.

Web publication rights: The buyer can publish your piece multiple times on the Internet, but not via e-mail, downloadable e-books, or CD-ROM.

Archival rights: The buyer will place your words in an archive for a limited or unlimited period of time. A common example is a daily newspaper archive that makes articles available in print and online for a limited period of time and then moves them into an online database.

Electronic distribution rights: The buyer may resell your words to other electronic outlets. And they won't be sending you a cut of the profits.

All electronic rights: The buyer may do all of the above. But unless otherwise indicated, they own only the electronic rights, not the print rights (but you should clarify this).

Work for Hire

This is the least advantageous position for a writer. Basically it means you are writing as an employee of the publication and your employer retains all rights and the original copyright to your work. This is similar to working on a con-

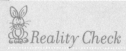

Reality Check

What can you expect for pay from various kinds of publications? Here's a basic breakdown of three levels of pay you can expect for a full-length article:

Types of Publications	Approximate Pay Per Article, in U.S. Dollars
Local Magazines, Regional Magazines, Internet Publications, and Weekly and Monthly Newspapers	0-100
Trade Magazines, Glossy Regional Magazines, Daily Newspapers	100-500
National Magazines	500-2,000

tract basis. You are paid for your efforts, yet all ownership of what you create goes to the person paying you, who can give you credit for your writing—or not. They can also make additional money by selling your writing without ever paying you another dime. Think twice before accepting these terms as a freelance writer. This is generally the position writers are in when working as a freelance copywriter for businesses. They work "for hire." Check out these sources for more information: Gordon Burgett, *Sell & Resell Your Magazine Articles* (Writer's Digest Books, 1997); Moira Anderson Allen, *Starting Your Career As a Freelance Writer* (Allworth Press, 2003).

To Sell or Not to Sell?

In the beginning stages of your career, the bulk of your energy will go into getting your writing in front of editors. So stay loose when it comes to negotiating and try not to get hung up on it. How good you feel in negotiations often reflects the number of submissions you have in circulation. If you have the promise of more work, then you are in a comfortable position to negotiate—as in, "Take it or leave it." If you don't have any other prospects, it's easy to slip into desperation mode ("You want to publish it? Really?"), followed quickly by resentment mode ("What? You think I should give you all rights? You've got some nerve!"). By far the most empowering step you can take when it comes to rights is to be informed and know *your* rights. That's why it makes sense to join a professional organization like the American Society of Journalists and Authors (www.asja.org). They maintain a helpful free e-newsletter on contract rights news at www.asja.org/cw/cw.php.

Here are some typical scenarios in which beginning writers find themselves and how to handle them:

The publication makes an offer for less than one hundred dollars. First, there is little point in negotiating terms with publications that pay less than a hundred dollars for feature-length articles. Generally speaking, they simply won't offer any more than that, so why haggle over a few bucks? Also, these publications tend to pay you a flat fee regardless of how many words you turn in. So don't quibble about word count, or pay rate, or anything else. Make your assessment based on how nice of a clip you will get and how much you want to write on the topic. As always, your objective is to get the best clip you can, complete your work as quickly as you can, and move on to higher-paying publications.

The publication wants all rights. Even though this may be one of your first deals, remember that you are not selling your baby. You are selling words that you put together on a page. If you have no clips, and you're writing for a familiar audience on a topic in which you want to cultivate expertise, consider selling all the rights. You can always write more pieces on the same topic; you will just need to start from scratch. As we have discussed, if you have strong clips and expertise under your belt, you can command higher rates of pay without having to sell all rights. If you feel conflicted, get the input of a more experienced freelance journalist.

You get stuck in low-paying publications. Don't get stuck in a rut of aiming for lower-paying publications. It's easy to get in the habit of staying too long in your comfort zone and avoiding the discomfort that arises from stretching yourself as a writer and a negotiator. Is it shrewd to get that clip, or are you just taking the easy route? The answer to that question will point you in the right direction. If your clips can sell you to a higher-paying, wider-reaching publication, then it's time to consider moving up. When you are ready to work on your financial and negotiating muscles, here are two sources for study: Kelly James-Enger, *Six-Figure Freelancing: The Writer's Guide to Making More Money* (Random House, 2005); Michael Meanwell, *The Wealthy Writer: How to Earn a Six-Figure Income As a Freelance Writer (No Kidding)* (Writer's Digest Books, 2004).

When in Doubt, Ask a Pro

If there was ever a good time to solicit input from a pro, it's when you are an inexperienced negotiator. State your request simply. Describe the situation thoroughly. Tell the more experienced writer how you feel about the negotiation. They will ask for more information if they need it. Run their response by your gut. Does it feel like the best advice for you at this point in your career?

Then make your decision. And remember, it's normal to feel uncomfortable when you are doing new things. A professional will respect that you've gotten this far on your own and probably not mind helping you at all.

Painless Ways to Get More Rights or Money

You should *always*:

- Read the fine print on all of your contracts and cross out any clauses you don't agree to before you sign them.
- Ask for the best contract available—some editors have a better contract ready if you ask for it.
- Respond to an offer, at minimum, by asking, "Is this the best pay rate you can offer?" And if it is, add, "It's lower than what I usually get for an article that takes the same amount of time and effort," and see what happens. It never hurts to calmly stand up for yourself and your work.

Wendy Burt's Accountability Sheet

You can stay on track with your goals by using this accountability sheet that Wendy Burt has been using for years. If you fill out this form once a week, it will help you assess your progress and drop your lowest-paying gigs.

DATE:

PART I: REVIEWING AND EVALUATING YOUR WEEK

1. On a scale of one to ten, how was my writing production this week?

exercise

2. Unfortunately, a *negative* investment of energy went to (In other words, how did I waste time this week?):
3. The most meaningful thing I did this week was:
4. Regarding my goals, I was pleased that I spent time …
5. How many of my five weekly goals did I accomplish? (Set them for next week.)
6. Did I do my "dread"? (The one thing I really didn't want to do.)
7. Did I succeed in dropping one unproductive habit?
8. Did I succeed in adding one more productive habit?

PART 2: PLANNING A NEW WEEK

1. My "stretch" for this week (What's a stretch for me?):
2. This week's dread (C'mon, you know what it is):
3. This week I will drop (Which activity is impeding progress?):
4. This week I will add (Which activity will increase my productivity, profitability, or professionalism?):

MY GOALS BETWEEN NOW AND THE END OF THE YEAR

Goal #1: One action to take toward this goal this week:
Goal #2: One action to take toward this goal this week:
Goal #3: One action to take toward this goal this week:

THIS WEEK'S ACTIONS

1.
2.
3.
4.
5.

Set Satisfaction-Based (and Monetary) Goals

You already know how to make money in this business: by satisfying editorial needs. So let's talk about how you will satisfy your personal needs by connecting what you write to your greatest sources of satisfaction. Your inspiration may be family, in general, your kids, specifically, cherished friendships, a love of literature, or any number of meaningful topics. The key is: You get to decide. Assume that you will base your career choices on earning money *and* personal satisfaction, and then entertain some of these possibilities.

Your best bet is to push yourself to dream a little bigger while also being realistic. If you're not certain what's realistic and what's fantasy, simply focus on what you would like to see happen. But don't just think about yourself. Who will you dedicate your writing career to? Your spouse? Your children? Your parents? Perhaps to members of an audience you wish to address? This is the dreaming part. It's not the action part. (Just so we're clear on that.) However, clarifying your intentions around your work life can take you further, faster, and keep you going when things aren't going exactly the way you'd like. Consider the following questions:

Where would I like to be in my writing career in ten years?
Where would I like to be in five years?
In four years?
In three years?
In two years?
Next year?

SET ANNUAL GOALS

No business can succeed without setting goals and then making a plan to reach those goals. The place where your financial rubber hits the road of reality is your annual goals list. If you don't have one, you will accomplish much less than if you do. You just did some daydreaming about your long- and short-term goals, but now it's time to get serious. Focus on where you want to be financially one year from today. Yes, you are going to need to commit to a number—you now know enough to be able to make a realistic assessment of what you can do. Just give it your best guess, and then take that guess seriously. Go a bit higher than what you think you can accomplish, but stay within the realm of possibility. In addition to Wendy Burt's accountability sheet on pages 199–200, which is the best strategy for reaching goals I have ever seen, try these as well:

1. Write down your goals as a statement of commitment, sign it like a contract, and post it where you will see it. From here on out, ask yourself daily, "What concrete steps am I taking today to reach my goals?" This will help you make your overall goals more tangible, so you will take them more seriously.

2. Expand your goals to include context: What will your future office look like? How will you spend or reinvest the money you make according to your values? Will you buy a nicer computer, a new car, or even just decent pens? Will it bring you satisfaction to pay your kids' tuition or dental bills? What will your career mean to your family?

3. Create a Goal Board—a bulletin board where you post images, quotes, and objects that remind you of your goals and inspire you to meet them. Creativity expert Lee Silber suggests that you use your bulletin board as a touchstone to help you decide whether time for a task is relevant to a goal or not. That way you won't be easily sidetracked.

4. Make one of your goals to make mistakes and lots of them. You can't grow without making mistakes. That's just reality. If you have to know everything before you dare to act, you will never act spontaneously on things that must be done. By

committing to making mistakes, you give yourself permission to not only fail, but also succeed. Here's a mistake manifesto that you can read and sign, or adapt to suit yourself.

MISTAKE MANIFESTO

I, _____, do solemnly declare that I deserve to have a writing career. By signing this document in the presence of my charges, their attendant stuffed animals, and a few assorted dust bunnies, as well as my spouse and anyone else who cares to bear witness, I officially vow not to give up my ambitions for the sake of a few (possibly silly) mistakes that I either have already made or am yet to make. Upon signing my Jane Hancock, I will get to work advancing my writing career from this day forward, one teeny-weeny step at a time.

I commit to make mistakes and lots of them. I commit to more trial in an effort to someday make less error. I will not sign this document, in blood or otherwise, without swearing allegiance to the actual act of writing and not just talking about, dreaming about it, or whining about it. I promise to do my footwork, to submit my work, and to stick my neck out whenever and wherever reasonable, though the winds of self-doubt, self-pity, and questionable self-esteem may occasionally rear their ugly, vile heads.

On this day, the _____ of _____, I pledge allegiance to my writing career.

Signed:

_____

Did you sign? I hope so! If so, maybe you'll take actions that will lead to some great mistakes—and not as many as you might think—in the coming year.

18

Run With Your Assignment

> *In some ways, I believe anyone can do it, and yet they don't set aside the time or they don't do the revisions, or they do it and it sits, or they send it out to one place and when it gets rejected they don't send it out again.*
>
> ~ ELIZABETH RUSCH, MOTHER OF TWO

The query is sent. The offer is accepted. You have squared away the assignment and negotiated payment, and you are ready to write! Typically, time will have passed since you worked so hard on that query and prewrote your feature. You may even have to reread your notes just to remember exactly what you proposed (I mean, you've sent out a lot of other queries since then, right?). Give yourself a big pat on the back and then get ready to write!

Feature Writing Tips

1. Refresh your memory. The good news is that because you pre-wrote your feature before submitting it, you have a container bursting with writing starts and notes that will help start your draft. But before you go writing off into the sunset, pull that magazine back out and remind yourself how your feature is going to match up. Here's what to look at:

- the length and language used in feature titles
- the length and language used in feature subtitles
- the size of feature subsections
- the language used in features in general
- the tone and style used in features

Studying other people's work isn't meant to rein in your creative approach. On the contrary, it is meant to get you back in the mood. You may be tempted to jump back into a feature from memory, and that's fine for writing notes to yourself. But you'll be surprised by the things you may not have previously noticed you need because, before, so much of your energy was focused on your query. You may also want to pull out whatever market notes you collected on this publication (guidelines, editorial calendar, media kit), as well as your current assignment.

2. Keep writing projects orderly. I use a paper sorter with twenty-four compartments for my projects in process. That way I can store everything (papers, back issues, a book, and even my small audio cassette player and tapes) within reach and in good order. Folders and even folder pockets may not be big enough to contain everything you gather. But the paper sorter works great. And after an assignment is completed, even materials from the largest projects fit into folder pockets that I store in a filing cabinet.

3. Break it down into subsections. Draft your feature using whatever method feels most comfortable to you. If you feel overwhelmed by the depth or scope of your feature, break it down into subsections that correspond to a research folder. You will end up with several folders of research for one feature this way, but that works well, because when you sit down to work, you can focus on one section at a time. You can rearrange material for clarity as you tighten up your drafts.

4. Play the "Did I nail it?" game. When you get to the almost-done point, go back to your sample magazine and, *again*, align your title, subtitle, section titles, callouts, captions, sidebar headings, and anything else to those that characterize the magazine. You can play the "Did I nail it?" game to see how tuned in you are to your editor's likes and dislikes. Read the titles in the magazine aloud, and then read aloud your title idea, subtitle, captions, etc. You will hear the difference if your choices don't match up. Adjust accordingly.

5. Your strongest lede. Forget formulas for crafting ledes. Here's a better strategy: Write your best lede last. It's easier to write the guts of your feature first and worry about the lede later. For example, let's say you have just completed writing your feature. You now know what the reader does and does not need to know, the questions the reader will ask and how you will or won't answer them, and the key points the reader will take away from what you wrote.

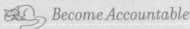
Therefore, you are in a great position to write an irresistible lede. The whole point of the lede is to lure the reader into your writing so they can receive the value you've worked so hard to provide. Ledes hook the reader, and hook 'em good. Here's an example lede:

> It's easy to forget to make time for yourself when you have to juggle an important meeting, three kids in three different schools, a traveling spouse, and commitments in your community. So how come other moms always seem to "have it all" and still have time to work out, read the latest bestsellers, and spend time with their friends?

I was not yet a mom when I wrote this lede, but I knew enough moms to be able to imagine the frustration a mom might feel. But to simply say that would be "telling," not "showing," so I described it instead, thus placing myself in the shoes of the reader. To heighten the drama of an otherwise not-terribly-dramatic list article,

I posed a question that a frazzled mom might ask herself. The result? The reader wants to read on to find out the solution to a problem she can identify with.

No matter what, your lede must:

- intrigue, tempt, or seduce your reader
- be written in your strongest narrator's voice
- evoke or echo your entire piece in only a few words

This is no easy task. A lede is not a gimmick. It's not a trick that writers play on readers to fool them into reading their writing. I offer you these simple keys to writing ledes as strong as you will ever need:

- Write your lede last, or toward the end, and polish it until it gleams.
- Grab your reader's attention with the juiciest stuff you've got going for your piece.
- Plant yourself firmly in your reader's shoes and don't budge (at least not until you can perceive the value of what you've written from the reader's perspective).
- Kick your voice all the way up, not just a notch—this is not the time to be subtle (although an understated lede can certainly be effective, if it's a natural extension of the storyteller's voice).
- Go for the gut of your reader—the only way to determine this is to know your story and your audience.

Occasionally, I hear about a writer who has to have a perfect lede before she can go on to write the rest of a feature. But more often, a writer has a solid middle before she has a beginning or end. The solution is to try three ledes and go with the strongest one. Write the three quickly when you finish the guts of a piece and see which works best the next day.

And don't forget your caboose! You need a strong finish for your feature. Although some editors seem to like conclusions, while others just chop them right off, be sure to offer one, just in case. Tying your conclusion back to your lede is a simple way to get the job done.

6. Get some stylebooks. Remember that wish list? Now you will better understand why you need to add stylebooks to it. Even though they may not be exciting to collect, stylebooks sure come in handy when you are finalizing drafts of articles. Whether you are trying to choose between *lay* and *lie*, wondering if a comma or semicolon is more appropriate, or unsure whether to capitalize or not, stylebooks have your back. And they are available new, used, or at your local library:

Scraps

Consider composting your old work as you go along. Hold onto everything you write at least until you know you no longer can squeeze any value out of it. Here's how: Keep an extra document open in your word processing program. It should be named the same as your original document plus the word "Scraps." Anything you cut that you think you might want to use or reference later can be tossed into this document and saved right next to your working draft.

Occasionally, pull up all of your "Scraps" documents. Skim them, either on your computer or as hardcopies, and see if you can generate any new ideas on old topics. Sometimes the material in your Scraps document is interesting, but irrelevant to the old topic. Consider recycling still-viable topics into something new, especially if the topic is in your area of expertise.

For all writers: William Strunk, Jr. and E. B. White, *The Elements of Style*, 4th ed. (Allyn & Bacon, 1999)

For magazines: *The Associated Press Stylebook and Briefing on Media Law*, ed. Norm Goldstein (Perseus Books, 2002)

For books: *The Chicago Manual of Style*, 15th ed. (University of Chicago Press, 2003)

Appropriate Perfectionism

It's time to polish your words. Look at your latest draft while asking the following questions. Circle your answers.

THE LEDE		
Y	N	Does my lede cut right to the chase of what the article is about?
Y	N	Does my lede pull the reader in? Hook the reader by helping him identify with the topic??
Y	N	Have I used my lede to focus the rest of my article or essay?
Y	N	Does my lede transition smoothly to the body of my piece?
THE BODY		
Y	N	If an article, does the body of my piece have a clear rhythm/organization?
Y	N	If an essay, does the body of my piece have a compelling narrative throughline?
Y	N	If an article, is the body of my piece broken up into easy-to-read chunks?
Y	N	If an essay, does the body of my piece evoke the senses with accurate and specific details?
Y	N	Are my descriptions succinct and relevant?

Y	N	Are my anecdotes, facts, allusions, and resources succinct and relevant?
Y	N	Have I eliminated every extraneous word?
Y	N	Have I eliminated redundancies?
Y	N	Are my verbs active and punchy?
Y	N	Have I checked my facts to make sure they are current and accurate?

THE CONCLUSION

Y	N	Do I have a conclusion that ties back to my lede?
Y	N	Does the the reader now know something that she didn't know before reading the article?

IN GENERAL

Y	N	Have I honored and maintained my voice and writing style?
Y	N	Has the piece been read by one to three people whose opinions I respect?
Y	N	Have I given this piece my very best effort?
Y	N	Have I proofread the piece for grammatical errors?

Writing Career Ups and Downs

Remember the board game Chutes and Ladders? If not, you will probably become reacquainted soon. Your writing career will follow a similar up-the-ladders and-down-the-chutes pattern. No doubt you'll discover that your career makes steady progression, punctuated by triumphant ascents and discouraging setbacks. What I have noticed is that the "ups" tend to follow smart choices and good preparation. There is no such thing as "luck" in the publishing industry; there is only the fruition of cumulative efforts. What follows are some typical writing career fluctuations, in the style of the board game that was one of my childhood favorites. It's by no means comprehensive, but should offer you plenty of fair warning:

SQUARE 1: GOING UP!

Join a professional writers association. Learn relevant, current industry insights and break in faster.

SQUARE 4: GOING UP!

Sift and mix some of your separate audiences into more narrow audiences (for example, parents who are also fitness buffs or entrepreneurs). Land assignments that are fun and easy for you to write and lead to a specialty.

SQUARE 9: GOING UP!

Schedule a monthly "Breakfast with Champions" (meeting with already published writers). Learn from the people who are in the know and can refer you to industry insiders.

SQUARE 16: GOING DOWN!

Ask a well-known writer for a personal referral, when she is unfamiliar with you and your work. Whoops! Now you are embarrassed *and* referral-less!

SQUARE 21: GOING UP!

Encourage another writer into action, not ego. Together, you try to get away from attempting to be "great writers" and simply try to be productive writers. You'll be there to cheer her on when she needs a push and give her permission to do the same for you!

SQUARE 28: GOING UP!

Help a first-time published writer promote his book by writing an Amazon.com review, requesting his book at your local bookstore, and sharing news of the book and how to purchase it with appropriate friends. Reward: Author connects you to his agent with a personal recommendation!

SQUARE 36: GOING UP!

Identify your writing and publishing needs, goals, and areas that need improvement and address them with specific classes, resources, and books. Overcome the blind spots that flag you as a beginner or keep you from steady work.

SQUARE 46: GOING DOWN!

Spread gossip about a writer friend you secretly envy. You lose her trust and the confidence of your other friends. Be more honest about your envy and keep it in check.

SQUARE 47: GOING DOWN!

Unwillingness to start at the bottom and work your way steadily to the top causes you to to cut corners, skip steps, and take shortcuts. Your submissions and queries end up in the literal and virtual garbage. Be as conscientious and informed as possible, and don't skip steps.

SQUARE 49: GOING DOWN!

Decide to mass e-mail your queries without doing due diligence on each publication and editor. Figuring you will be recognized for the great writer you are without needing to waste your time doing silly marketing, you instead earn a spot in those editors' "Flaky Writer" files.

SQUARE 51: GOING UP!

Make yourself a cover, query, and manuscript checklist and use them religiously. You keep as many of your manuscripts and queries in play as you can, and begin to land increasingly higher-paying assignments and reprint multiples of your past writing!

SQUARE 62: GOING DOWN!

Your house is a mess, you don't care how you dress, and your final drafts could use a makeover too. But you don't care; you just want to get it done and move on. Downside: Editor keeps sending your work back for rewrites while making a mental note not to offer you the next assignment she had earmarked for you.

SQUARE 64: GOING DOWN!

You're too proud to ask for help. You're going to do all of this all by yourself—and can't understand why it is taking you so long to establish any kind of sustainable success.

SQUARE 71: GOING UP!

You tell your assigning editor, "Sorry, I can't take on another assignment right now. I'm all booked up, but thanks for the offer. I hope you'll keep me in mind next time." Bonus: Spend quality time with the family getting and giving much-needed hugs and kisses!

SQUARE 80: GOING UP!

Follow your gut and submit your work to a prestigious contest. Win first place and cash reward! Family vacation, here you come!

SQUARE 87: GOING DOWN!

You make up "true stories," falsify quotes, facts, and statistics, and lie when you need an extension, rather than develop a personal code of writing ethics in which you can take pride—and you get caught. Article gets yanked. Public humiliation. Lesson: Track facts and sources and give credit where credit is due.

SQUARE 93: GOING DOWN!

Scared writer: Too shy to seek input. You are intimidated by experts and editors and can't get beyond list articles and tips.

SQUARE 95: GOING DOWN!

Too proud to take low-paying or free gigs on topics you like because you think you're a pro (although you have zero clips to show for it). You quit after six months of not being able to land assignments because editors want to see examples of your published work (clips).

SQUARE 98: GOING DOWN!

You take on too many low-paying assignments in swift succession, get burned out, and can't understand how anyone could make decent money in a profession that values writers so little. You quit just when you could have moved up the ladder to the next natural level for your writing.

SQUARE 100: WIN-WIN-WIN!

You work hard, leverage your experience, gain confidence and wisdom, earn the recognition of your professional peers, and are a respected colleague of editors and agents!

IV.
Poise

19

Wear All the Right Hats

> *I know it sounds a little harsh. To be successful, which for me means to accomplish the goals I have set, you must be willing to get rid of the things in your life that are not producing results you can be proud of.*
>
> ~ SHERI McCONNELL, MOTHER OF FOUR

W riter mamas wear many hats. As a freelance writer, you are a creative being, but you are also a businesswoman and an entrepreneur. With these roles come a whole variety of responsibilities—for example, taxes—that add to your already overloaded day. But moms are supposed to be really good at multi-tasking, right?

While there is some truth to that, let's face it—that story has been played so much that a mom starts to feel like if she's not a multitasking fool, something must be wrong with her. So if your mind feels like it's permanently set on spin cycle from all that you've got going on, don't be too proud to call for help. Every mama has her gifts—don't let your choices be dictated by what some other mama can handle.

Check out the hats listed in this chapter. Try them on. See how they fit. But don't feel guilty for *even one second* if you start to wonder if you couldn't use some professional help in any of the hat departments—especially the one where you have to pay The Man on April 15. (And if you're even wondering whether you need an accountant, you probably do.) Take good care of your business and your business will take good care of you (and your family).

The Accountant Hat

Even if you don't make a lot of money in your first year of writing for publication, it's important to treat your writing like a business from day one. You may think that you've got plenty of time before you need to start keeping careful track of money spent vs. money earned, but don't wait because, if you do, I guarantee you will have lost track of some of your all-important deduction receipts, and that is just perfectly good money wasted.

You may feel like there is little point in treating your writing like a business instead of a hobby, unless or until you make more than a certain amount of money. But that is foolish if you are serious about working steadily and consistently until you make what you would consider a decent income. Through the eyes of Uncle Sam, there is no magic amount of money that causes the IRS to view you as a business; rather it's how you conduct your business—no matter what your profits (or losses)—that grants you professional status.

Here's a simple system to set up from the first day you start to write that will help you track the important documents you need to keep. Use it, and you'll have everything you need when you sit down with your accountant, bookkeeper, or tax preparer (which I strongly suggest you do, unless you or someone close to you knows how to file taxes for a small business) at the end of the year.

Important Documents to Save and File

If you can print, file, and save these documents as you go along, you will save yourself a lot of headaches and regret.

Submissions: Keep Every Single One. You will be tempted to skip saving your submissions (meaning every doc you send in for publication consideration). For example, you may think, "Nah, this silly little tip isn't that important—besides, it didn't get accepted." But get in this habit: submit, print, file. Make it a weekly routine. From the IRS' point of view, your submissions prove that you are in business. If you don't have them, you can't prove anything. So get in the habit of keeping them or you will be cursing yourself on April 14. (Especially if you aren't backing up and you have a computer crash. Yikes!)

Contracts, Assignments, Rejections: More Proof You Get Paid to Write. Along the same lines as tracking all your submissions, you need to keep careful track of all your contracts, letters of assignment (aka letters of agreement), and rejections. The reason is the same as with submissions. These documents prove that you are actively in the writing business, as opposed to trafficking rare coins.

Invoices and Payments=Money Earned. Certainly by the time your income hits the one thousand dollar mark annually, you should start filing your writing income and expenses as a business. Until now you may have viewed your efforts as a hobby (even though I suggested not to), but once you cross that all-important income line, you need to keep careful track of your income and expenses in a simple profit and loss sheet. Until that time, keep payment stubs or check copies stapled to the appropriate invoice as a way of visually indicating that you got paid, so you will know how much income you are earning.

You will have everything you need when the time comes to do a profit-and-loss analysis (a bookkeeper can do this for you or you can learn to do it yourself) if you use folders to contain your expenses (receipts) and income (pay stubs or photocopies of checks). When you're just getting started writing and publishing, you can create a quarterly spreadsheet, but once you start making more money you will want to track your income and expenses as you go.

To create a basic profit-and-loss statement, write the name of the income or expense in the left-hand column, and then put the categories, date, amount, income or expense, and all of your tax deduction categories across the top. Most computer software will let you enter your income and expenses in any order and then sort it by date. You will want to stay on top of your income and expenses so that you can make quarterly estimated tax pay-

"⏰" *Does It Pay to Sell Reprints?*

Writers love to talk about all the ways to recycle writing. However, in my experience, most editors, even those of small or regional publications, prefer content written specifically to suit their readers. And they will usually find writers who are willing to take lower pay to generate that original content before they will take a reprint on a non-regional or non-reader-specific topic that has appeared elsewhere.

Of course, there are exceptions to this rule, and I have sold plenty of reprints. But the fact remains, when I asked writer moms what percentage of their income came from reprints, the response was only about ten percent. An original idea—whether in query form for an assignment or many smaller pieces submitted with cover letters—brings in more income than unoriginal work (reprints) sold again (and in some cases again, and again, and again).

So ask yourself this: Does it make more sense to invest a whole bunch of time and energy into finding markets for your reprints or into digging deeper into your specialty? To my mind, discovering and cultivating a niche is a smarter way to go when your time is scant.

The time to explore selling reprints is once you have a specialty, or even a few specialties. I suggest you wait until then. In the meantime, reuse *the research* you've already gathered from one feature (or any type of piece) to pitch to a non-competing market (this is called reslanting). You will make more money, and expand your expertise and visibility as well.

ments once you start earning. When you do, consult a tax professional—the fee is tax-deductible.

Tax Deductions=Money You Reinvest (and Don't Have to Pay the IRS). You are the keeper of your own books, and an accordion file and updated tax information are what you need to prepare for a meeting with your bookkeeper or accountant. I recommend ordering *Foolscap & Quill's Writer's Pocket Tax Guide* as a preliminary guide. It's only ten dollars and walks you through tax preparation line by line, including the all-important Schedule C (Profit or Loss from Business, Sole Proprietorship).

More Documents to Track

Uncle Sam doesn't care about these, but you do. Tracking them is as easy as marking a folder and keeping a three-ring binder handy.

Correspondence Related to Assignments and Contract Amendments. Always file any correspondence that alters the terms already laid out in a letter of assignment or contract. The IRS doesn't require these documents, but you should keep track of them in case a discrepancy ever arises with your submitted work. For example, say you sign a contract for an assignment with a June 14 deadline, but your child gets the chicken pox, and you request a weeklong extension. Keep the correspondence granting your request and add it to your contracts folder, just for the record.

Clips and Manuscripts-in-Process. Purchase a nice three-ring binder with plastic sheet protectors to preserve your clips. It's also a good idea to keep track of the unpublished writing on which you've spent time but haven't yet published. Otherwise, it's all too easy to forget about it. You may prefer to keep unpublished work in a folder so that you can access it easily. Another possibility is to keep work-in-progress in a stacking file of folders on your desk, with the understanding that you don't file folders away until the manuscript has been submitted. However you choose to organize your work, try not to lose track of your pieces while in the fledgling stages—it's so easy to start something and never finish it.

Here are a few examples of possible deductions to give you a better idea of what to collect before you meet with a professional (consult a licensed tax professional to be sure you don't miss a single acceptable write-off):

office supplies
office rent or home office expenses
office utilities
legal and professional fees

> class and conference fees
>
> postage and copying
>
> computer and office equipment
>
> software and books
>
> subscriptions, dues, and annual fees
>
> travel, meals and entertainment
>
> fuel (don't forget to track mileage)

A Brief Word on the Home Office Deduction

Does it make sense to designate one space in your house or apartment as your home office? Yes, it does! If you follow the current home office specifications, you get to write off a portion of your rent or mortgage. But fair warning: Be sure to get the details in advance so you can set up shop correctly. When it comes to taxes, you simply can't fudge it. *Foolscap & Quill's Writer's Pocket Tax Guide* will give you the information you need to set up your home office appropriately.

Other Freelancing Hats

Remember in chapter two when you looked at your roles and chose keywords that best described you? There wasn't just one word that described who you are; there were four, or ten, or twenty. You are many different people, all wrapped up in one great package.

You'll play many different roles in your career, too. When it comes to the many hats that writer mamas wear, just remember that your hats are here to help, not hinder, your business. The ability to shift gears in your business helps create harmony and increases success. Here are some of the hats you may find yourself wearing:

General Manager: In charge of planning, delegating (even if only to the family), watching the bottom-line.

Marketing Specialist: Identifies clients, analyzes markets, studies how other writers market themselves.

Copywriter: Generates copy for all business communications including cards, Web site, catalogs, and brochures.

Graphic Artist/Printer: Responsible for laying out and printing documents; also designs Web sites and makes copies.

Production Manager: Creates work schedule, oversees quality control, brainstorms spin-off services.

Mail List Supervisor: Tracks and updates e-mail lists and newsletters.

Customer Service Associate/Administrative Assistant: Fields calls, answers questions, makes offers, orders office supplies, writes and sends correspondence, buys and sends professional gifts.

File Clerk: Sorts and files important papers.

Bookkeeper/Accountant: Sets up and updates ledgers, approves and pays bills, balances checkbook, prepares for taxes, stays current on tax laws, makes deposits.

Computer Expert: Keeps all business documents backed up on a daily basis, registers Web pages, stays up to date on technological advances that affect business.

Communications/Networking Coach: Stays current on industry policies, joins and attends professional associations and events, gives back work in kind or money to like-minded causes.

Publicity Director: Uses press releases to alert media and professional organizations of professional advancements.

Proofreader: Makes sure documents are error-free before they are sent out.

Does this sound like a lot of hats to juggle? Just for fun, buy yourself some *actual* hats to help motivate you to do the tasks you enjoy least. And don't forget to reward yourself for doing the business tasks you don't enjoy. After you do some unavoidable administrative or bookkeeping work, take yourself out for coffee or buy yourself some colorful new pens. Positive reinforcement works well here—and don't forget, those pens are a tax deduction!

Try on the Editor's Hat

You've come a long way, mama. Far enough to be able to borrow someone else's hat. How about trying on the editor's hat for a change? Pick a publication off the rack—maybe even one you've never seen before—and play editor for a little while. Writer Diana Burrell likes to take herself out to the local bookstore, buy herself a cuppa joe, and sit down with a pile of magazines in front of her. She then puts on her editor's hat and forgets herself altogether.

She plays a little game in which she pretends she's an editor in an assigning mood. That's right: By studying a magazine, Diana Burrell has developed a knack for reading an editor's mind (or at least trying to).

exercise

What would happen if you tried this technique? Forget your long list of ideas for a change. Forget what you know and what you want to write. It's helpful to forget yourself sometimes and just focus on how to provide articles that will be a perfect match with what an editor needs and wants. The point when you can switch points of view between editor, reader, and writer is the point at which all your preparation, practice, and professionalism start paying off. You might be ready to try this technique sooner than you think. You might be ready now. Why not give it a go? Then switch back from your editor hat to your writer hat and pitch those ideas! You will find that you draw on everything you've learned so far when you pitch this way.

Seventeen Ways to Avoid Writer Mama Burnout

From time to time, writer mamas feel the burn of being overworked. Too many deadlines and not enough fun make mommy a dull (and crabby) girl. Here are some really simple reminders to help get you back on track when you start feeling fried, so you can nip mommy burnout in the bud.

1. **Say "no" to assignments until you find your smile again.** The creative cycle has downtime built into it. Have you been doing enough nothing lately? Gather the family onto the bed or couch and just veg for awhile. Watch TV, have a picnic in bed, watch movies—anything to get out of work mode.

2. **Seek succor: Recognize you are on overload.** Talk about it to someone supportive. Ask for input. Make a list of your options. Consider the possible outcomes if you ease up. Consider the possible outcomes if you *don't* ease up. Then ease up.

3. **Spend time walking in nature.** Walking or exercising, even in short spurts, will refresh you. Go alone or take the kids. Try a trip to the local zoo, or another activity that gets you out in the fresh air and reminds you that there are species outside of the publishing business! Do something nice for yourself, especially something you "shouldn't" do, like get a massage, pedicure, or pretty piece of jewelry. How about a mom's day at the spa? Buy yourself fresh flowers. How about a bouquet in each room? Seriously, you deserve it! And if you create a pretty environment for yourself, work might not seem so bad.

4. **Take care of yourself.** Drink lots of fluids, take your vitamins, and eat a healthy diet. You get your kids to do it, but you may have forgotten yourself. Time to pony up on self-care.

5. **Join or form a writer mama support group.** Make it sometimes work and sometimes social, or half-work and half-social, or whatever everybody wants.

6. **Quit a group that is draining you or taking up too much time.** Avoid people who are draining you or who try to make you feel bad about yourself. Do something nice for someone you love and truly appreciate. Recruit your kids and do something nice together.

7. **Find someone who is supportive of your career ambitions.** Talk to a career counselor, spiritual counselor, or therapist about your inner challenges on an ongoing basis. This includes the times when you don't think you need to talk, like when you make great strides. This will help you avoid a backlash or guilt.

8. **Go on vacation.** Even if it's the middle of the week or not the same time everyone else goes on vacation. When you need a break, you just need one. Maybe a day away from home or a night in a hotel by yourself? Can you imagine? Scandalous!

9. **Take a break from writing for a day or two.** Keep your computer turned off, if you can possibly swing it. Banish cell phones. Tell technology to go away. See if you feel better. If so, you may be suffering from technology overload. Try not to be so plugged in all the time.

10. **Do something else creative.** Pottery, mosaic, scrapbooking, or jewelry making are fun. Other creative outlets can revive your weary muse. How about something with the kids? Finger painting, blowing bubbles, or sidewalk chalk are good possibilities.

11. **Go to the library or bookstore.** But this time, go without an agenda or list of research for a change. Browse. Hang out. Lose track of time.

12. **Read for pleasure.** Read to your kids. Read books you used to like as a kid. Don't read anything for work. Read magazines you'd never consider writing for.

13. **Volunteer to do something that has nothing to do with writing.** Caveat: Don't overdo this. Volunteering is a slippery slope, especially if folks know you are "available." Know that you can say "no."

14. **Kick back.** Take more long showers and hot baths. Do housework at a leisurely pace. You might enjoy it. Now there's a switch!

15. **Forget you are "a writer."** Try being "just a mom" again. A wife or a partner. A daughter, a sister, a cousin, or a friend.

16. **Have a backwards day.** Have everyone in the family do everything backwards. Stay in bed. Eat pizza for breakfast. Read the paper backwards. Try it, and see what happens.

17. **Recover an area of expertise that makes you feel excited and alive.** Go in that direction with your writing career when you are ready to get back to work.

20

Establish Expertise in Your Field

> I'd advise all writers, if you think you might ever want to write a book, to consider building up your reputation on the topic as far in advance as possible. It'll help you sell the book and sell it for more money if you're already recognized as an expert in the field or if you have a built-in fan base.
>
> ~ JENNA GLATZER, EXPECTING

W ith all you have to manage as a busy mom, there's a good chance that it will take years before you are ready to apply some of what is discussed in this chapter. However, the day will surely come when you have honed your marketing, writing, and professional skills to the point where you are not merely ready, but itching, to tackle the next step: proposing a nonfiction book. And even if you are not close to being ready when you get to this chapter, keep reading! Now is the best time to start planning how to increase your chances of success as an author in the future (and it's always going to be in the future until you go ahead and try!). If you are ready to propose a book, you will find these last few chapters, covering the transition phase between freelancer and author, particularly helpful.

Before you land a nonfiction book deal, and even before you write up the proposal to pitch your book concept, you would be wise to first establish and build your expertise.

What's an Expert?

An expert is a person who has a great deal of knowledge, skill, training, or experience in a particular field or activity. Obviously, there are degrees of expertise. It's not like you can simply drink a glass of fine wine or eat a gourmet meal and become an instant connoisseur! However, you can become an expert in a wider variety of areas than you might think. And just as all writers were once unpublished, all experts were once not experts. You can begin where you are today, with what you currently know, and develop a plan for increasing your knowledge, skill, training, and experience in the future. In a world seemingly full of experts, it may be tempting to dismiss the title as arbitrary, but when you set out to build your expertise, don't make any mistake:

None of the women mentioned in this chapter were born experts, and while they were quietly laying the foundation for their platforms, nobody knew who they were. But they did the legwork needed to be qualified experts in their respective fields.

Be alert to the lure of experts who "pop up" seemingly out of nowhere. Expertise does not happen in a lightning bolt. True experts may emerge into the public eye quickly, but make no mistake about where they came from or how long it typically takes for them to lay their foundation; knowledge typically follows a long gestation period.

The only reliable way to know who is a true expert and who is merely a self-proclaimed expert is the "ring of truth." And the only place to register that ring is right in your own gut. In addition to staying alert to "instant" experts, beware of confirmed experts who fall off a straight and narrow path. Sometimes, formerly sane, solid professional writers get carried away. And that's a shame. If an expert's story has the ring of truth, proceed, but stay alert. And if you feel like you are getting a snow job ... maybe you are.

Legitimate experts don't earn that moniker by chance, but rather by conscious intention. And you can't just go calling yourself "expert" and expect others to listen. Without the respect and trust of others, you're just posturing.

But Don't Experts Need an Advanced Degree?

Certainly many experts have advanced degrees. But the idea that doctors, lawyers, and various professionals are the only kinds of experts among us is too limiting for writers who have an eye on steady, conscientious career growth. Many areas of expertise are created by the very people who pioneer the role. Martha Stewart had a career in finance and even tried real estate before she found her stride as a caterer. After seven years of career experience, she conceived the idea for her first book, *Entertaining*. Today there is an entire section of the bookstore by the same name.

An author may also be a process expert in teaching, customer service, or research, for example. She might be a product expert in books, toys, or art. And she might have a specialty within her expertise. For example, a party planner might specialize in children's birthday parties.

Within the broader title "expert," there is room for variety, and we're not going to try to tackle the whole range of possibilities. Suffice it to say, expertise isn't just about what an author puts in a book; it is invisible real estate owned, packaged, marketed, and sold in as many guises as you choose by you, the president and CEO of Expertise Productions. And you can't make expertise happen overnight. It's a process just like everything else.

Why Do You Need to Be an Expert?

Developing your status as an expert expands your options as an author. Back when we were talking about article writing it was another story. You'd come up with an idea for a magazine, and then either expand that idea into an article and send it in, or pitch it, land the assignment, and then submit the article. With freelancing, except for an occasional rewrite, once you deliver the final version of an article, your job is done.

But when you become an author, the commitment is much larger and more ongoing. And many more people are involved. Potentially, there are agents, acquisitions editors, content editors, designers, proofreaders, and publicity agents, just to name a few. The best way to be an equal partner in the myriad of relationships that come with authorship is by standing on a firm foundation of expertise—past, present, and ever-evolving. Why not begin today?

"Produce Yourself"

One of my favorite things to say to writers is, "You have to produce yourself." But what does that mean? You can find out by looking back with me at the credentials of three nonfiction authors who have worked long and hard to build their reputation and vision and make the most of their expertise. I think by remembering that all of these women had to start somewhere just like you, you'll begin to have a clearer idea of the difference between expertise and specializing (which was discussed in chapter twelve).

If you write an article on comfort, you are not a comfort expert. If you write an article on writing, you are not a writing expert. If you write an article on getting out of debt, you are not a debt-recovery expert. However, if you make a conscious decision to dedicate years of your life to the pursuit of a deep and wide foundation of knowledge on these topics, then you might be on your way to pursuing expert status.

These three women have earned their expertise in their fields not because they write for a particular audience or about a particular topic (as a specialist does), but because they have made large investments in the credentials, experience, and professional exposure that back up their expert status.

Mary Hunt—Professional Cheapskate
(www.cheapskatemonthly.com)
Over the course of thirteen years, Mary Hunt worked her family out of over 100,000 dollars worth of unsecured debt. The result is a getting-out-of-debt mini-empire spearheaded by her subscription-based newsletter *Debt-Proof Living* (formerly called *Cheapskate Monthly* and available

in various formats). Hunt has penned numerous traditionally published, self-published, and e-published books, not to mention making good use of paid online tools intended to convert spendthrift readers into "cheap-skates," who follow in her footsteps.

Jenna Glatzer—Writing and Getting Published Expert
(www.absolutewrite.com)
Jenna Glatzer started AbsoluteWrite.com in 1998 and has since published eight books, written articles for hundreds of national, regional, and online publications, and contributed to eight anthologies. One of the highlights of Jenna's career has been working with Celine Dion on her authorized biography, *Celine Dion: For Keeps*. But this expectant mama wasn't always flying high. She suffered from and overcame agoraphobia, and edited a collection of essays on the topic called *Conquering Panic and Anxiety Disorders*. Absolute Write has allowed Jenna to create a community of writers of all stripes who come to Absolute Write's Water Cooler for a social outlet and to share industry information. She also launched *Absolute Write* newsletter and *Absolute Markets* paid newsletter and maintained a subscription base of 75,000. After eight years, she sold her business in order to create space for her first child.

Jennifer Louden—Comfort Expert
(www.jenniferlouden.com & www.comfortqueen.com)
Jennifer Louden became an author with *The Woman's Comfort Book* and then wrote a whole series of "comfort books" including *The Couple's Comfort Book*, *The Pregnant Woman's Comfort Book*, *The Woman's Retreat Book*, and *Comfort Secrets for Busy Women*. Her books have been translated into

nine languages. Today, in addition to being a best-selling author, Jennifer is a personal coach, workshop facilitator, retreat leader, and keynote speaker. She published her first book in 1992, and has been establishing her expertise ever since. Naturally, since there are no advanced degrees or professional tracks available in "comfort," Jennifer's professional history has been more self-styled than some. She refers to herself as a "social commentator" and "cultural visionary," which is not surprising since the need for her expertise may not be self-evident to those outside her target audience. Since she has been cultivating her expertise for over a decade, it's only natural that her work has evolved alongside her career and the perceived need for what she offers.

How Do I Uncover My Expertise?

My students often wish to broaden their horizons and develop expertise in areas other than the ones they already have.

If you can identify with this feeling, this might be a good time to delve into a book designed specifically to help you discover the body of knowledge that inspires you enough to become self-motivated. *The Artist's Way* by Julia Cameron, *A Life in the Arts* by Eric Maisel, and *Marry Your Muse* by Jan Phillips are all good books that can help—but don't think you have to stop writing and go "find yourself." Why not put the books on your nightstand along with whatever else you are reading while you continue to work on writing and getting published? Maybe in the meantime, you could give the expertise you've already acquired through jobs and education a second chance before ruling it out completely.

Identifying Your Expertise

It's smart to continually build on the expertise you already have. And once you have chosen an area of expertise, here are ways to cultivate that skill or knowledge so it will grow into a virtual garden of possibilities (as it has for the expert examples in this chapter).

1. Identify your strengths and weaknesses in the bigger picture of your field. Then:

   - Use your strengths to set you apart and establish what you offer that others don't.

   - Use your weaknesses to point you toward the skills that need improvement (maybe one of your colleagues in the field can help you in these areas).

2. Identify what you are most passionate about in your field (this may be a skill—such as coaching—or a topic you want to dive into more heartily or specialize in). Then:

   - Use your passion as a springboard to make some plans—do something with what you already know. (What can you do? We'll talk more about that in the next chapter.)

   - Use your resistances as an indication of where you might trade services with other professionals—for example, hire a bookkeeper in exchange for writing some publicity materials for them or helping them with their Web content.

3. Identify your biggest fears about the arena you are about to enter. Then:

   - Get out of isolation by joining associations, clubs, and online communities for folks just like you—you've got to grow and keep growing to get and stay known.

   - Use the expertise you already have to position yourself as an expert with services to offer—for example, you might teach, coach, or speak on your topic, while continuing to work on your writing and getting published (more on this in the next chapter).

How Do You Establish and Maintain Expert Status?

Why not create an expertise development group? Sometimes there is no substitute for a buddy or group that you start up for the sole purpose of helping the members or buddies establish and develop expertise. Encourage each member of the group or partnership to take concrete steps to increase their expertise. If you need new proficiencies, look into degree programs, certification programs, and professional training schools. To maintain your professional status, join professional associations in your field, subscribe to trade journals, stay current with what's going on in the media, compile a library of relevant resources, and attend professional conferences and workshops. Think continuing education, and don't neglect yours if you want to keep your expertise fresh and keep yourself and others engaged in your topic. (We'll talk more about attending writers conferences in chapter twenty-two).

Perhaps a focus on developing and maintaining expertise could become part of your Writer Mama Circle or current writers group? Seriously, what would happen if you got a small group of aspiring writers together and everyone in that group conscientiously nurtured their expertise alongside their writing careers? Good things would happen, that's what!

Why Can't You Just Write?

You can! And you should until you feel ready to dedicate time and energy to the worthwhile endeavor of establishing expertise. The reason this chapter is included in this book is because it's not uncommon for freelancers to become frustrated with "the system." Frustration is the number one motivator for writers to uncover their expertise. Typical freelancer frustrations may include not being treated with enough respect and courtesy, low pay rates, hard work, and long hours for minimal lasting returns. And perhaps one good solution is to take steps towards establishing your expertise and turn your career towards authorship. I'm not going to kid you, though: A whole new boatload of challenges comes with a shift in career direction.

Certainly, if you begin to feel that you want to throw up your hands and abandon your writing career for something "easier," you may want to evaluate your expertise tank. Is it full or empty? As your perception of yourself changes from freelancer to expert, the way others treat you will also change. Before you know it, you'll be an another expertise success story. But just as the skills in sections one through three of this book required practice and lots of it, this shift from viewing yourself as a freelance writer or freelance journalist to expert is going to take an investment of your time, energy, and money.

Today Expertise, Tomorrow Platform

Why a whole chapter on the subject of expertise? Because it would be difficult to understand the topic of the next chapter without an understanding that the foundation of any decent marketing platform is good, solid expertise—the kind that can only come over time. When we move to the next chapter we'll look at how a marketing platform expands the definition of expertise beyond simply *what* you know to *how you leverage what you know* to make yourself more visible. Writers make themselves more visible every time they publish an article with a byline. So if that's what you're doing, then you're on the right track. We'll discuss other good ways to start getting known in chapter twenty-one, "Get Your Name Known."

Uncover the Expertise You Already Have

Okay, now it's your turn. I happen to have it on very good authority that you are already an expert. What? No one told you? That's okay, let's work on it right here. I find that the majority of my students have trouble identifying and claiming legitimate expertise that they have already spent time, energy, and money developing. Start with your past and gather everything you can come up with until you get to the present:

What did you learn how to do because of ...

- your childhood?
- your formal education?
- your profession(s), jobs, or careers?
- your continued/self-guided education?
- your relevant personal or life experience?
- any projects you've started?
- your unique and distinct point of view?

I suggest you get out your journal and spend some time freewriting in response to each of these prompts. When you're finished, ask yourself this question and then answer it ten times while you're warmed up from writing: "What I'm really an expert on is _____."

Imitate the Attitude of Writer Mama Pros

Moms are usually more familiar with what it takes to develop career confidence on a job than in a home-based business. Before motherhood, many were lawyers, nurses, graphic designers, service professionals, and public servants. Even if you carry over professionalism from another arena to your home-based writing business, you might be surprised to learn about the qualities that set prolific and publishing writer mamas apart from wannabe writer moms. Here are twelve qualities of highly successful writer mamas and businesspeople everywhere:

1. **Determination.** Natalie Goldberg is famous for saying that it takes great determination to be a writer, and she could not be more right. Most of those who have persevered as writers over the years have done so because of resolve; some might even say stubbornness. Think about the areas of your life in which you possess great determination. If writing is not yet one of them, steep in imaginary conviction for a while. Remember the feeling so you can tap into it as you go along your merry writing way.

2. **Creative Thinking.** Moms are blessed with the ability to think in multiple ways. Pregnancy, birth, and motherhood do something to the way our brains work. Whereas we may have once been able to only think quite logically and reasonably, after becoming parents our minds seem to form additional patterns of thinking: circles rather than lines, holistic rather than black and white, more playful, like our kids, rather than too serious. This is actually helpful to

writer mamas. Your ability to think in lines and circles is an asset, not a liability. The key is to know when to go nonlinear and when to proceed in a good, orderly direction. A balance between the two is your best bet.

3. **Ability to Prioritize.** Prioritizing speaks to the writing mom's ability to know where she is and what needs to happen next. It means you can ask the question, "What is *the* most important thing I need to do next in order to complete this project?" And then do it. This way, you don't need to see the future as much as navigate your way through your work.

4. **Discernment.** This is the ability to consider options you may not have planned for. Willingness for the mom writer is not the same as being everything for everybody; it's the ability to say, "Hmm, that's an interesting proposition. What would happen if I took this assignment?" It's the ability to weigh and measure options and go with the one that feels the most promising in the moment even if the wisest response is saying, "No thanks." Discernment comes from taking time for reflection to get a clear "read" on the situation (and don't forget to trust your instincts).

5. **Self-Directedness.** You are a self-directed mama when you don't need someone else telling you what to do in order to accomplish your goals. You determine on your own what needs to be done and how to proceed. Intuition is definitely an important part of the self-directed mom's decision-making process. Responding to their internal compass is how writer mamas get from where they are today to where they'd like to be in the future.

6. **Responsiveness.** Successful writer mamas are a pretty communicative bunch. In order to join their ranks, practice being available, on a reasonable basis, to the outside world. Of course, you can't be available twenty-four/seven, or you would never be able to concentrate on and complete important tasks. But there's no need to be a hermit—unless you have a deadline looming; then you

might want to think of yourself as a hermit-in-training (who still keeps in touch regularly with the family).

7. **Detachment.** Home is often the hub of a family's emotional life, so it can be a challenge not to take everything that happens in your home office personally. Another rejection? They do seem to happen. An editor's comment on your work feels like a zinger. Are you sure? Let it go, or ask for a second opinion. Editors usually go out of their way not to step on writer's toes.

   On tough days, when things start to close in around you, take a deep breath—and pull back. In the writing life there are plenty of opportunities to take things personally—or not. Once you let the annoying stuff go and get busy again, you'll realize that you can't spare the time to obsess about the slight stuff (or at least the stuff that feels like a slight). Be respectful and you'll get respect. If you don't, remember that you can't control others. So don't dwell on it.

8. **Resilience.** Writer mamas need to learn how to hit bottom and bounce back. Sometimes you are going to be up, and sometimes you are going to be down. Sometimes you may be both in one day or even one hour. Just like daily life, the writing life is full of ups and downs. The pros learn to ride the ebb and flow without hanging out too long in either extreme.

9. **Consistency.** Writing is a regular task when you're a professional. Writing success happens when effort meets opportunity steadily over time, but it takes effort to create opportunity. At the end of the day, it is consistency that sets the flash-in-the-pan successes apart from the lifetime achievement award-winners. Sure, the flash-in-the-pan writer might get some temporary glory, but the mama with staying power is the one who reaps the most satisfaction.

10. **A positive attitude.** Seasoned writer mamas have a natural exuberance that comes from hard-earned success. Why shouldn't they have something to smile about? And, even if you're not a success yet, who would editors rather work

with again: the writer who meets every challenge with an upbeat attitude or the one who meets them with grumbles and excuses?

11. **Composure.** A little different from detachment, composure isn't about pulling back; it's about staying sturdy and riding the waves. This one gets easier over time. In fact, composure is often gained from persevering through trying experiences. It's about responding to success as well as to disappointment by staying somewhere in the middle. Exuberance is great. Venting frustrations feels good—true. But composure is grand.

12. **Conscientiousness.** Show me a professional writer and I will show you a person who takes quiet pride in her work, with the patience to go over her words again and again until they are polished just right, until—as one of my students once said—"It sounds like a song with every word exactly right." On the flip side, a lack of conscientiousness will lead to a lack of opportunities, dissatisfied editors, and a hollow feeling inside. Don't be hard on yourself. Just do the best you can and keep on striving for personal excellence.

21

Get Your Name Known

> *Whenever you get an interview, article published, or some other platform goodie, post it on a wall of your office, preferably in a frame. It builds mojo and convinces your subconscious to keep the momentum going.*
>
> ~ SUZANNE FALTER-BARNES, MOTHER OF TWO

I f you are a writer mama with ambitions of becoming an author, the one thing you must do is start getting known now. Agents and editors at publishing houses are specifically looking for writers with an established following to sign for nonfiction book deals. Your visibility and influence increase your chances of selling your book in a crowded and competitive marketplace. With so many writers vying for reader attention these days, what's going to make your book stand out from the rest? Your marketing platform, that's what!

What's a Platform?

One definition of the word *platform* is a flat, raised area of ground, and that's a good way of visualizing what a platform means to publishing industry pros. Your platform includes your Web presence, any public speaking you do, classes you teach, media contacts you've made, and any other means you currently have for making yourself and your future book known to a viable readership, including articles you publish on topics in your area of expertise.

Have you achieved a certain level of expertise that others recognize? If so, you have already started laying the foundation for a platform that will put you head and shoulders above "the competition" (meaning others proposing book ideas to agents and editors). Simply put, your platform is what communicates your expertise to others. One thing all of our experts from the last chapter have in common is that they have a public presence. That's why when they write a book on their area of expertise, people who know their reputations listen. Jennifer Louden writes "comfort" books, Jenna Glatzer writes books on writing and getting published, and Mary Hunt writes books on getting out of debt. People purchase their books because all three of these authors already have a reputation. In a sense, their books are just a natural extension of what they already do.

Sample Platforms of Successful Writer Mamas

The Personal Perspective Platform

(Young, Unwed) Mother Outsider: Ariel Gore. Ariel Gore established her nonfiction writing career on the basis of her experience as a welfare mom, teenage mom, urban mom, and college-educated mom. She felt that the way she and other moms on welfare were treated and perceived deserved a voice, and she became a voice for that point of view by launching a zine on the topic called *Hip Mama*. As a result of her efforts, her story became her niche, her niche blossomed into a readership, and every word she's written since is uniquely Ariel. Right up to her six-figure advance for *The Hip Mama Survival Guide*.

(More recently Gore has moved on to memoir, and recently fiction, but she still writes and publishes nonfiction. Hers is a good example, in my opinion, of how a career in nonfiction can successfully expand into other genres, and how writer mamas are only limited to writing about motherhood if by choice.)

Ariel Gore's Books

> **Fiction:** *The Traveling Death and Resurrection Show*
>
> **Memoir:** *Atlas of the Human Heart*
>
> **Nonfiction:** *How to Become a Famous Writer Before You're Dead*; *Whatever, Mom*; *The Mother Trip*; *Hip Mama Survival Guide*; *The Essential Hip Mama*

The Fill-a-Niche Platform

Literary Mama Duo: Andrea Buchanan and Amy Hudock. I remember the flurry of excitement among some of my students when *Literary Mama: An Online Magazine for the Maternally Inclined* launched in November 2003. The feeling might have been put into words like this: "Finally, a site for moms like us"—referring, of course, to moms who write intelligent, thoughtful, truthful, literary words and then cannot get them published. Although the award-winning zine was, and continues to be, a group effort pulled off by many women who pitch in, two of the more visible authors associated with the site are Andrea Buchanan and Amy Hudock. They run a Web site that attracts thousands of visitors each month and this is the key to platform. Publishers want to know that you have a built-in audience for your book or books and a way to directly get in touch with them. Take a look at how starting an online zine for literary moms is helping them both build literary careers.

Andrea Buchanan's Books

> **Essay Collection:** *Mother Shock: Loving Every (Other) Minute of It*
>
> **Anthologies:** *It's a Girl; It's a Boy; Literary Mama: Reading for the Maternally Inclined*

Amy Hudock's Books

> **Anthology:** *Literary Mama: Reading for the Maternally Inclined*
>
> **Arts & Literature:** *American Women Prose Writers: 1820–1870*

Professional Experience Platform

Finger on the Pulse of Busy Professional Moms: Maria Bailey. If you are a working mom, you may have heard of Maria Bailey. You may even read her online magazine, *Bluesuitmom.com*, which is loaded with articles, tips, and expert advice for moms who tread the stretched-thin line between motherhood and career. Maria has four children, a husband, and a growing media company, BSM Media, that specializes in connecting companies with moms.

In addition to her online magazine, Maria Bailey is the host of the nationally syndicated *Mom Talk Radio*, the publisher of the bimonthly magazine *Today's BlueSuitMom*, and the creator of Smart Mom Solutions, a product line for busy moms. Can you think of any reason why a publisher wouldn't love her? Imagine the size of her Rolodex! Besides, she has multiple media channels to reach readers and advertise herself, her services, and her books. And, finally, she has a nice, long, extremely professional track record, which equals clout.

Maria Bailey's Books

Nonfiction: *Trillion-Dollar Moms*; *Marketing to Moms*

Why Think Platform Now?

Little Ways to Drop Your Name

- Purchase your name's URL. Hold onto it for the cheapest price available, so you can upgrade when you're ready to build a Web site.
- Use e-mail signatures to direct people to your Web pages.
- When you're ready to build a real page, try using a free one-month trial. But don't forget to pay it before the expiration date, or you could lose what you've built.
- Use a real e-mail address with your name in it and nothing else silly. Not christinathewriter@earthlink.net, but christinakatz@earthlink.net. (That really is my e-mail address, if you'd like to say hello.)
- Create an e-mail list and add names to it that you collect everywhere you go. Actively invite people in your audience to join your list or group. Be sure to offer them something that they will enjoy.

Everything you've learned in this book so far has helped you understand the difference between an author with a marketing platform and a freelance writer who may not necessarily have or need a platform, so this seemed like a natural place to bring it up. Your marketing platform is not of a great deal of inter-

Questions About Platforms Answered

Q. I have a great idea for a nonfiction book. Why would I need a platform?
A. Most nonfiction book deals start with a short pitch, followed by a longer book proposal, followed by a contract negotiation, followed by a period of drafting the book, followed by a period of editing the book, followed by a period of promoting the book. Now, it may sound like a platform would not be required until the very end of this process, but most editors are looking for a platform before you even sit down and write them a query. In fact, if your book concept is not backed up by as wide and tall a platform as you can build, your chances of being the writer selected to write a book on your topic are thin indeed.

Q: Yes, but if I can get an agent interested in my idea, I won't need a platform, right? Because the agent will do all of the selling?
A: Unfortunately, wrong. Both agents and editors are looking to sign contracts with writers with a large sphere of influence. Generally speaking, the larger your sphere of influence, the larger dollar amount you can expect in your contract. So you need to think big when you think about reaching people: millions, or at least many thousands. Of course, you are not going to start a Web site tomorrow and have ten thousand hits on your page, but you have to start somewhere. So think strategically, then make a beginning, and build up your self-promotion efforts over time. A good formula for self-promotion is to accomplish one small self-promotion task a day. But before you start, you need to think about audience, a body of material, and your strongest areas of interest.

Q: But I've got two deadlines and a toddler with the flu. I've already got my hands full! Do I really need to start working on a platform now?
A: Well, you don't *have* to do anything. And, in my experience, a platform needs some time to gel and become strong and wide enough to take root in order to make an impact on editors and agents. So, yes, even if you do nothing but start exploring possible platforms or even start studying what other authors are doing platform-wise, take some steps in the direction of your possible platforms. Start small and let your platform grow and evolve over time, just like everything else in a writing career. And let your platform be something satisfying, if not fun. Don't develop a platform you can't stand, although I think that would be hard to do anyway.

Q: After you publish a book, do you have to build a whole new platform?

A: Your platform is uniquely yours forever. You can have one platform that grows, expands, and splits in two or ten, or you can start two separate, unrelated platforms. If you were to dramatically switch audiences or topics, you might wish to create a separate platform. Suzanne Falter-Barnes has done this with her expertise on creativity and getting known. They are related, but not exactly the same—at least not from her audience's perspective—so she has two separate, but complementary, platforms.

est to magazine, newspaper, and online editors. Those editors don't care how well known you are (unless of course you are *very* well known, as in well known enough to get into *O, the Oprah Magazine*), as long as you do a good job on their article and deliver it on time. But book agents and editors want to know how much clout you have. They want to know if other people—not just your friends and family, but a wider circle of influence—listen to you, pay attention to you, look to you for advice. They'd prefer an audience in the thousands, at least (for a start).

Tools for Getting Known

What does a platform mean for moms who are hiding in the minivan, scribbling furiously while waiting for the kids to finish soccer practice, or sequestered away, fingers tapping across a keyboard? How can you be visible and sequestered at the same time? That's a good question, and the answer isn't as difficult as you may think, thanks to the Internet. Whether doing things online or by more traditional means, you can increase your platform. Do you:

- Have a Web site?
- Maintain a blog?

- Publish a newsletter?
- Host a radio or podcasting show?
- Produce a television show?
- Write a regular column or hold a contributing editor spot?
- Have an established business name or reputation?
- Teach or facilitate workshops?
- Make media appearances?
- Speak or keynote?
- Consult or coach?

If so, you have a platform. If not, but you'd like to, put yourself in training to do one of these things soon.

And always remember this: Everything you post on the Web is a trail of virtual breadcrumbs that media-folk and their assistants follow when they want to check you out. So be very conscious that what you are putting out in the world represents you in the best and most professional light.

exercise

Start Something

What can you start tomorrow? Seriously, the sooner you start something, the longer it will have to grow and gain momentum between now and when you need it.

I started my online zine *Writers on the Rise* (originally called *A Writer's Companion*) as a way of keeping in touch with my former students. At first I just had a simple e-mail newsletter. Then I upgraded it to an online zine and got other writers involved.

Next, I upgraded to a more visual layout, adding photos and headshots of contributors. I keep growing it, right along with my writing career. Who knows what I'll do next! I just keep doing the next best thing for the zine and the readers, and I have fun doing it. In fact, I always welcome the break from other types of work to pull together the monthly issue of *Writers on the Rise*. Why? Because it's my baby (well, my other baby).

What could you start that makes sense to you and your career? Is there a niche or a need you can fill? That's a good place to start. And then just roll with it from there and let it grow and evolve over time.

Develop Multiple Income Streams

One important habit to get into when you attempt to straddle the distance between writing short and writing long is to watch your bottom line. When you start working on longer writing projects, the pay may be higher, but the payout schedule may stretch out over time. A smart way to bridge the gap between checks is to do or sell other things alongside your writing as a method of creating multiple income streams.

Here is a list of possible services to consider and the name of a writer who is already successful in that line of business:

Public speaking: Kelly James-Enger gives presentations on writing and fitness topics at colleges, libraries, and conferences. In addition to a successful writing career that has resulted in four nonfiction books and two fiction books, Kelly is a certified personal trainer and has been published in over fifty national magazines. (www.becomebodywise.com)

Manuscript evaluation: Elizabeth Lyon offers editing services and manuscript evaluation as part of her platform. She runs Editing International, which offers services including editing, coaching, group instruction, outsourcing, and writing, provided by herself and her associate editors. Elizabeth has written five nonfiction books and presents at writers conferences around the country. (www.4-edit.com)

Teaching workshops or classes: You can teach classes independently, through an institution or organization or online. I teach e-mail classes through my Web site

Writers on the Rise. I've taught adults live at a community college and independently via e-mail, each for three years. Last year, I branched out into conference presentations and speaking. This is my first book. (www.writersontherise.com)

Editing (freelance, contract basis, or as employee): Wendy Burt offers freelance editing to custom magazines along with her writing. The two services complement each other, so clients can hire Wendy to both generate content and manage it as well. Wendy's experience as an author of two books has led her to edit books for other authors and to counsel authors on everything from book proposals to agents and foreign rights.

Consulting in your area of expertise: Jennifer Louden, the comfort expert, offers consulting services to companies like Proctor & Gamble, Johnny Rockets, and Spandex Fiber. She has also worked with associations like the National Council of the State Boards of Nursing. She has appeared on the Oprah Show, CNN, and CNBC and is the author of six books. (www.jenniferlouden.com)

Copywriting for businesses: In addition to writing for national magazines and teaching a writing class via e-mail, Linda Formichelli offers copywriting services to corporations. She's penned brochures, newsletters, press releases, ad copy, radio scripts, and slogans for companies around the country. (www. lindaformichelli.com)

Co-authoring/Ghostwriting: Jenna Glatzer offers ghostwriting and co-writing services. She's written three nonfiction books for writers and one children's book of her own and has ghostwritten or co-authored five additional books (which sometimes carry her name—With Jenna Glatzer—and sometimes don't). (www. jennaglatzer.com)

Self-Publishing (newsletters, e-books, and self-published books): C. Hope Clark publishes four newsletters for writers (paid and free), eleven e-books to help writers find funds, and a self-published book, *The Shy Writer*. She also offers online chat sessions and writing contests for writers. (www.fundsforwriters.com)

Naturally, when you create an additional service as a part of your writing career, it becomes part of your platform. But don't feel pressured to launch a secondary branch of your writing business until you feel ready. You may wish to wait until the kids go to school, or until you have some help around the house or with watching the kids, before run the risk of spreading yourself too thin. And like everything else, building any kind of business takes time and thrives best when set on "slow and steady."

22

Count Down Days to a Conference

> At the New York conference, I had a chance to reconnect with old friends and make some new ones as well. When I'm around smart, talented, interesting, funny writers, I realize how much I've missed working with other humans all day. I'm like a sponge absorbing all that wonderful—and necessary—contact and connection.
>
> ~ KELLY JAMES-ENGER, MOTHER OF ONE

Writers conferences are excellent opportunities to connect and hang out with fellow writers. Conferences offer workshops, talks by published authors, question-and-answer sessions, face-to-face meetings between authors and agents/editors, schmoozing sessions, and more. A conference offers writers who don't get to New York, L.A., or other cities heavily populated by editors a chance to offer their expertise to editors in the form of a book pitch (which we will talk about in more detail in chapter twenty-three). There really is a conference for everybody. Some conferences last for one day; others last for ten. They can be general (for all kinds of writers) or very specific (for romance, western, or mystery writers). Some have attendees in the high hundreds; some have less than a hundred. Usually, the meetings are annual events but some organizations have several gatherings a year.

Even if you don't wish to pitch a book, the educational immersion available at a writers conference is worth the cost. They can be pricey, even running in the hundreds of dollars. But don't let your fondness for small price tags deter you from attending a writers conference this year. Get one on your calendar and commit to showing up prepared and ready to network. A writing conference is well worth the investment, and if you plan ahead, you just might meet the key person who can help you land a book deal or teach you how to submit successfully to your ideal publication.

Visit Shaw Guides (http://writing.shawguides.com) to find a conference near you. You can search by month, by genre, by state, and by country. And don't be afraid to e-mail the conference contact person directly to ask questions, seek referrals, or inquire about volunteering. The sooner you get a conference on your calendar, the sooner you can take advantage of discounts and get the most out of every opportunity available to you.

Meet and Greet

The most important people you can meet at a conference are those you wouldn't otherwise meet—and when you work from home most of the time, that's just about everybody. Here's a quick rundown of who's there:

Agents: These are key players in publishing who keep close tabs on industry trends, developments, and opportunities for writers. They represent writers and their work to editors at publishing houses. While they cannot guarantee publication of a book proposal or manuscript, they can make the difference in garnering serious consideration. Agents are your best bet if you want to approach a large house with a book idea that has a large potential audience. At a conference, you should interact with them as much for what they can do for your prospective book, as what you can learn from their considerable expertise.

Editors: Acquisitions editors are the key decision-makers about which books will—and will not—get published by their particular publishing houses. Sign up for pitch sessions with these professionals first (if you have a concept that fits with their line), because you can always get an agent after you have a book deal offer in your pocket. Going straight to an acquisitions editor cuts down on lag time because there is no middle-person (agent)—and who can represent you and your idea better than you? If your concept is a specialized or smaller niche, go straight to the acquisitions editors at conferences.

Speakers/Featured Authors: The keynote speakers for a conference are usually authors who have achieved either best-selling status or have been

🐾 Meet Your Host: Your Writer's Association

Writing conferences are often hosted by writing organizations. Membership in professional writing associations is the single best method of advancing your career, if you take advantage of all of the opportunities offered. Some of the many benefits of membership in professional writing organizations include:

- Online networking
- Opportunities to announce your professional milestones
- Newsletters
- Online discussion boards
- Volunteer opportunities (some are long-term paid positions)
- Help with contracts

All this is typical in exchange for a small membership fee! Here are three kinds of associations to join when you are getting started that I recommend.

Your Statewide or Regional Writer's Organization (e.g., Willamette Writers). Willamette Writers is an organization for published and aspiring writers of the Pacific Northwest. Willamette Writers hosts an annual conference, monthly membership meetings, Young Willamette Writers, the Willamette Writers Conference, the Kay Snow Writing Contest, the Herzog scholarship, Books for Kids, a weekly e-newsletter of Oregon writing events, and a monthly newsletter. For all of this, the cost is only thirty-six dollars per year.

I've been a member of WW for almost two years and this alliance has been instrumental to the growth of my writing career. I pitched the concept for a book at the 2005 Willamette Writers conference—and you are holding it in your hands. Now *that's* a helpful organization. Join one in your area today!

A Women Writers Organization (e.g., The International Women's Writing Guild—IWWG). The International Women's Writing Guild, founded in 1976, is a network for the personal and professional empowerment of women through writing. Their mission is to engender and support "the joyful camaraderie that come from shared interests of a woman's writing community while at the same time establishing a remarkable record of achievement in the publishing world." Over one hundred books are published by Guild members each year. The Guild hosts eight national conferences per year, including one week-long conference. No portfolio is necessary to join. Annual membership is forty-five dollars per year. Visit www.naww.org for more information or to join.

A National Writers Association, (e.g., American Society of Journalists and Authors— ASJA). Founded in 1948, the American Society of Journalists and Authors is the nation's leading organization of independent nonfiction writers. ASJA offers membership only to freelance writers who have been published over a substantial period of time by recognized magazine or book publishers. Therefore membership in the ASJA "serves as proof to editors, agents, and fellow writers that you are a seasoned professional nonfiction writer."

If membership in ASJA is exclusive, why would I mention it here? Because setting your sights on membership in ASJA is an excellent goal for serious nonfiction writers who would like to join the ranks of approximately eleven hundred current members. According to Barbara DeMarco-Barrett, "The group was instrumental in [helping me] take myself more seriously. For one, I needed to collect more national clips before I could join. I had to work for membership, and when I was accepted into the fold, I felt that I had achieved something wonderful." Visit www.asja.org for more information.

consistently successful in the industry over time (not an easy feat). Keynoters are often just as accessible as other attendees at a conference and it can be wonderful to meet and interact with them.

Workshop Facilitators/Presenters: The people who speak and conduct workshops at a conference are generally also attending the conference along with everyone else, making them even more accessible than agents, editors, and speakers. Interacting with presenters is a great idea if you want to learn from their successes or ask for input on your particular idea.

I often say that these are the best people to talk to because their recent publishing successes can provide a writer who wants to pitch an idea with key tips and insights for getting a foot in the door at a publisher. If your idea is good, you might also receive a personal recommendation, which can help too.

Association Committee Members: These important folks work together to make writing conferences happen. Chances are good that they have put all they have into the production and promotion of the conference to make the experience wonderful for people like you. Also, these folks talk like no other group in the industry, so you always want to be courteous and friendly.

Association Volunteers: Volunteer opportunities range from planning/committee positions to folks who just show up for a half day at the registration desk. Other common duties include room monitor, silent auction coordinator, pitching registrar, and even conference chair. You can be a volunteer for some of the lower responsibility positions if you find the cost of admission to a conference to be above your budget. For the most part, volunteers are there for the same reasons as attendees, and are eager both to help and get as much out of the conference as they can. Be extra nice to volunteers too—most programming glitches, appointment pile-ups, and computer catastrophes are not the fault of a volunteer, though they will most likely be the person standing within grousing range.

Fellow Writers: There are gobs of these friendly folks all around at a conference. So even if you are shy by nature, try your best to stick out your hand and introduce yourself to as many of your fellow writers as you can. Keep an eye out for writer mamas. You will find them in lines for food, at keynote dinners, and workshops, at the registration desks, and in the restrooms. Talk to each other. And try to keep your conversations constructive and encouraging. Many writers are revving high on nervous energy at a conference, and some are just plain scared speechless. A friendly conversation can take everyone's mind off their conference jitters and make the whole event that much more pleasant for all.

Questions About Conferences Answered

Why Should I Attend?

If you're a mom who is serious about writing, get yourself to a conference as soon as your budget and schedule allow. Though you'll miss your little ones, you'll be surprised how much you enjoy yourself; your trip will feel more like a "mommy vacation" than work. If your kids are too young for you to be away for an entire weekend, try to at least attend one full day of a conference near you. (You can always increase your participation every year, as your kids become older and more independent.) The good news is that most states in the U.S. have writers conferences. If your regional writers association doesn't, you can probably still find one within driving distance. If driving is not an option for you, there are a few conferences worth flying for. Of course, the prospect of a plane ticket, conference ticket, and hotel bill add up, but maybe you can plan a family vacation around a conference—this way, that plane ticket or hotel bill is doing double duty. You can always slip away from family activities for a day or two to participate.

How Do I Know I'm Ready to Attend a Conference?

I constantly encourage writers to attend writers conferences. Most hesitate, as if these events are reserved for the elite few. They aren't. Conferences attract both beginners and seasoned writers and every level of experience in between. You are ready to attend a conference and there are no qualifications necessary. Even the ASJA (American Society of Journalists and Authors) conference, whose membership is qualified, makes their annual conference open to the public. The whole point of writers conferences is the sharing of timely information in the industry, so it's in the interest of brand-spanking-new writers as well as seasoned pros to attend in order to stay current on trends in publishing, technology, and craft.

But Are You Sure It's Really Worth It?

Stay away from naysayers and buddy up instead with a fellow writer or writer mama who is as interested as you are in getting as much as possible out of a conference. Then you can compare notes and share ideas and information with each other before, during, and after the conference. Think of a conference like a learning vacation. You are there to kick back, relax, and enjoy the company of your fellow writers. But also, opportunities abound at a writing conference and new ones present themselves every time you turn around. It's not just limited to what's on the conference agenda. There is a synergy and a serendipity that takes place naturally when you get a group of like-minded people together. Take advantage of it!

When it comes to writing conferences, like most things in life, you have to be smarter than your sources. Take comments that you see on message boards and in other online arenas with a grain of salt. Before attending a truly beautifully run conference with an excellent reputation this summer, I witnessed a conversation on a listserv that went something like this:

> Messenger One: Is it really worth it to attend that expensive conference?
>
> Messenger Two: Well, I went once and it was okay.
>
> Messenger Three: One of the presenters really annoyed me. Grouse, grouse, grouse ...
>
> Messenger One: Well, then maybe it really isn't worth my time or money.

This is not constructive advice about a conference. Like classes, books, and any other tool you employ to help you in your writing career, you will get the most out of a conference by preparing for it and soaking up its every benefit. If you don't want to take my word for it, speak to a few writers who have attended a conference you are considering in person. Call or e-mail and ask for referrals through the association that hosts it. I'm sure they will connect you with enthusiastic attendees who can help you get prepared and tell you what not to miss. It's always a great idea to take advantage of any insider information when it comes to events like conferences.

 ## What About the Kids?

Should you attempt to bring the kids to an annual writers conference? I would think about this very carefully. I once saw a woman at a conference with a baby in a carrier who was sleeping soundly and peacefully. I don't know too many babies like that, but if you have one, more power to you! Consider leaving the kids at home and taking a short break. If you are nursing, you might have the whole family stay at the hotel together and they can go swimming, go sightseeing, and eat out while you focus your energies on the conference. Don't bring the kids unless you also bring a spouse or sitter to go with them, as I have yet to hear of a conference that offers childcare. But hey, conference coordinators—if you want to make your events more mom-friendly, this isn't such a bad idea!

Get a Jump on Conference Registration

The best way to get the biggest bargain for your buck is to plan ahead. Conference material is usually available online or by brochure months before the conference. So do some research (start with the Shaw Guides) and find a conference that you could realistically attend. Do a thorough read on all the services and workshops being offered.

Join the association and get a discount. If you haven't already, the first step in preparing for a writers conference is to join the writers association that sponsors the conference (if possible). There is probably an incentive so that if you join you get a reduced price at the conference.

Register early for the conference. The sooner you join and the sooner you can get registered, the sooner you'll be in the loop for the latest information on upcoming conferences and events. Don't wait until the last minute or you may miss out on key preparation sessions or limited availability signup opportunities and crucial opportunities for agent/editor interactions, which often sell out before the conference. And make sure what you want and what you're signing up for are the same thing. Most conferences offer the à la carte method of registration (one day at a time) and the all-you-can-eat version (the whole conference).

Study up on who you'd like to meet. Take a close look at that conference brochure and decide who you'd like to introduce yourself to. If the agents, editors, and presenters have bios online, copy and paste their bios and headshots onto one piece of paper that you can print out and carry in your bag at the conference. This way you won't say, "Oh rats, I wanted to meet so-and-so!" after the conference, because you'll be able to recognize them by face.

Keep tabs on updates as the conference approaches. You will want to make alternative plans if any of your targeted agents or editors has to cancel. Keep a list of back-up agents and editors in case you need them.

Attending a writers conference is going to be one of the best things you do all year. Be sure to get it on the family calendar early.

Be a Prepared Conference Attendee

If you are like many moms, your clothing size before you had a baby may differ slightly—or more than slightly—from the clothing size you wear now. And if you're a new mom, you probably haven't had much of a chance to shop for yourself. So what's a mom to do when she opens up her closet the morning of the conference and there's not a thing to wear? Don't let this happen to you. Plan ahead so you can find and wear clothes in which you feel comfortable and confident and that make you feel fabulous, no matter what the size. And when it comes to what to carry, you'll want to pack light in order to avoid the dreaded strap indent in your shoulder that doesn't fade for a week.

WHAT'S A MAMA TO WEAR?

Wear "Business Casual." Since the attire is business casual and not business formal, you don't want to look like you are going to a luncheon on Wall Street or a funeral. If you wear black, add a splash of color with a pretty blouse or a cheerful scarf. Let your personal style shine through, but don't go overboard. Don't make the mistake of letting your clothes scream *I'm an artiste!* The same goes for revealing or overly sexy attire. A writers conference is a business event first and a social event second. Go for stylish business look instead, and be taken more seriously. If, like me, you don't usually wear makeup, just a touch can help remind you that a conference is a special occasion. And pay attention to what you wear on your feet. Chances are you'll be doing a lot of walking and standing, so even though you want your shoes to look as nice as everything else you are wearing, first and foremost, they should be comfortable. Most importantly, wear clothes that make you smile at yourself in the mirror and at others as you are passing them in the halls.

Finding Just the Right Outfit for You. Consider the season of your upcoming conference. When will the clothes you need be available on sale at your local department stores? This is the best time to shop. And luckily, retailers always have a bit of a jump on the season so chances are good you can hit a sale before the conference to fill in any gaps in your wardrobe. Nothing will make you feel worse than wearing clothes that used to fit you, but don't anymore. If you don't have any wardrobe gaps, congratulations! I know a few moms who don't—but I know a lot more moms who do. Don't sweat it! Remember that by dressing nicely you can still be one hot mama, making you feel good about yourself, which will affect how others look at you. If you feel confident, you'll be confident.

THE THINGS YOU'LL CARRY

Business Cards. You will want to carry cards for networking purposes, so be sure to order business cards about a month in advance. If you don't feel too shy, consider getting cards that have your headshot on them so that people who take your cards home with hundreds of others will recognize and remember you. There are Web sites that offer free cards in their own design, or allow you to create customized cards at reasonable prices. Keep them simple in design but feel free to be colorful or expressive, so long as those things communicate something about you and your writing. For example, a mom who wants to write a book on celebrity baby nurseries might include a sample photo on her card or an image of a fancy bassinet. Or she might just go for a straight business card with her name, address, e-mail, and Web site and print them on pastel-colored cardstock. Generally speaking, "Freelance Journalist" is more professional than "Writer." Be as specific as possible, but be honest. And, just like you target your bios, your queries, and everything else, keep in mind who the cards are for—you may wish to have one set of cards for networking with other writers and another for networking with agents and editors.

A Roomy Bag For Necessities. You need room for what you're carrying, as well as conference materials that you will pick up while you are at the conference. Don't forget your reading glasses, lip balm or lipstick, and anything you need to touch up your makeup or fend off blood sugar dips. It's helpful to have a business card holder. I picked up a pretty one at the hotel gift shop, but you can check online for fashionable ones. Carrying one saved me from having to dig around in my bag for cards, and also prevents cards from getting marred and bent. If all this adds up to more than you can reasonably carry, consider a rolling briefcase, as you are apt to do a lot of walking at any conference.

MORE GOOD THINGS TO BRING

Don't forget your cell phone or pre-paid calling card (but of course you'll turn *off* your phone or set it to vibrate while you're attending presentations, workshops, and pitching sessions).

Bring a change of clothes, even if you're there for one day and especially if you're wearing white. Carry Ibuprofen or Tylenol because headaches caused by too much mental stimulation are common. And carry a few bucks in cash in case you want to sit and chat privately in the bar or at a café with someone you meet. Bring plenty of pens, ink refills, and a manila envelope to keep the business cards you collect orderly. You may want a slim notepad or notebook, but most conferences provide this in your registration packet.

Simple snacks are another good idea. A small bag of nuts can be a lifesaver when all the food offered is high in carbs and calories. Don't worry about carrying beverages, there are generally plenty provided in the hallways. If you plan on snacking, or even eating lunch at the conference, then it is always a good idea to bring mints as well!

SAVE IT!

Be sure to keep all of your expenses for the conference—parking, food, book purchases, extra fees, agent/editor consults, photos, hotel bills ... everything—in a separate envelope, so you will be able to take advantage of all of your tax preparer's recommended deductions.

Save all the business cards you collect, even if you know it will take you a week to even look at them again.

Keep all the general conference materials for the rest of the year, because there is a good chance you will want to follow up with an editor or agent you meet at the conference at a later date.

23

Pitch a Nonfiction Book Concept

Before I started this conference volunteer gig, I really had a fear of putting myself out there with agents and editors and publishers. I would freeze before I sent e-mail letters, afraid that they would scrutinize every word I wrote. To some degree I was right, but in this role I interact so much with them that I now realize that agents and editors are just human beings too, doing their job, doing the best they can out there.

~ MARY ANDONIAN, MOTHER OF TWO

Nonfiction makes up the majority of books published today—just walk into your local bookstore and compare the fiction and non-fiction sections. Nonfiction is by far the largest part of the store, ranging from self-help, to health and fitness, to biographies and histories. And thousands of nonfiction books are published every year that never see bookstore placement—think of all the educational texts used primarily in schools or by homeschoolers, the university press offerings targeted to certain professions or fields of specialty, and the technical books published and promoted to a very specific audience. Nonfiction is a huge market with every imaginable niche!

Nonfiction can be divided into two categories: that which is creatively or artfully written (like narrative nonfiction or memoir) and that which is primarily information-driven (like this book). Sometimes how-to books or self-help books can be categorized as "prescriptive" nonfiction, which are books that tell you how to improve your life, relationships, finances, health, and so on. Many of the articles you write and publish will likely be service articles, so a prescriptive nonfiction book might be the best starting point for you.

Proposal or Concept?

A book proposal is usually a thirty- to fifty-page document summarizing the key points about your book concept that will persuade agents and editors of its salability. Obviously, writing something this lengthy takes a lot of time. Preparing a book *concept*, however, requires less of an up-front investment. You should use your time and energy for the proposal *after* a conference and *after* you've gotten input on your idea from industry experts, agents and editors, and published authors.

Input? Why would you want input? Don't you just want to get an agent to represent you? No, actually, you want to get the best possible agent to represent you, and you want to write the best possible book. That feedback is going to help you type up a stronger book proposal. If you don't get input, you'll probably end up rewriting your proposal anyway, so you may as well wait to start writing until you can incorporate all that you've learned into your proposal.

Most nonfiction books are pitched to agents or editors by mailing a complete proposal, and you should learn how to write a full proposal if you are serious about selling a nonfiction title. In the meantime, however, there is another option: This chapter tells you how to pitch your nonfiction book concept to an agent or editor you meet at a conference. And actually, the chances of an agent or editor asking for your proposal on the spot at a conference are slim (although it does happen occasionally). You are better off arriving at the conference with a tight, well-thought-out, and easy-to-describe book concept that can be easily shared and discussed in person.

Preparing Your Book Concept for a Conference

You don't need to bring a full book proposal to the conference to land a book deal; in fact, there are only really three sheets of paper that you need to share your book concept.

Mock Sales Copy for your Book Concept

Answers the question: "Why this book now?" Sales copy is what always accompanies a book in a catalog or on Amazon.com. When you read about a book before you decide to purchase it, you are probably reading sales copy. And in order to get a better handle on your book, the first thing you need to do is imagine the final product clearly enough that you can generate sales copy to go with the idea. Write your mock sales copy as though the book is already complete and for sale. For hints about how to write it, take a peek at the sales copy on other books by the same publisher and try to emulate it as best you can.

Typing up mock sales copy can also help you imagine what it might be like to have a finished book. When you're an aspiring author, the whole concept of a published book can seem abstract. Pinning it down with sales copy can make your book concept feel more real to you, which definitely helps when it's time to pitch it.

For example, when I pitched this book concept, I had my eye on Writer's Digest, so I looked at another Writer's Digest book: *The Pocket Muse: Ideas and Inspiration for Writers*, by Monica Wood. I copied and pasted the sales copy from the Writer's Digest Web site into a Microsoft Word document, studied it, compared it to other WD book descriptions, and then typed one up for this book. That description no longer describes the book you're holding in your hands, but that's my point exactly. Your "mock sales copy" may not accurately represent the final book; you just need it to represent the idea you have for the book today.

When you're done, how does it sound? Does it sound like a book you would buy? What makes your book concept especially timely and relevant in the world today? What problem does it solve? What are the benefits for readers?

A One-Page Bio Synopsis

Answers the question: "Why are you the best person to write the book?" Create two columns on the page separated by a half-inch gutter. On the right-hand side, list your platform credentials as they specifically support this book concept (including such information as relevant expertise, platform high-lights, big media appearances, and which reputable publications your work has appeared in). On the left-hand side use photos to illustrate your platform points (logos, images, your headshot, etc.). Limit the information and photos you provide to those that support you as the best person to write this book.

Author Julie Fast taught me this format for listing credentials to help spare agents' and editors' weary eyes since they often meet and speak with hundreds of conference participants in one weekend. It is definitely easier for anyone to scan a list with visual images than to review a traditional resume with all of its small type and irrelevant details. (To view a sample Visual Bio Sheet—I call it a one-pager—visit www.thewritermama.com.)

Market Notes That Prove an Audience and Need for Your Book

Answers the question: "Who's the market for this book?" Do research and make a one-page synopsis of the statistics and facts about the target audience for your book. Here are some questions you want to answer.

🎁 Run Agents and Editors by Your Mom Radar

A key thing to remember when you attend any writers conference in hopes of partnering with an agent or editor is that you are checking them out just as much as the other way around. You are looking for a partner, not a boss. Think of yourself as an equal worthy of their partnership. Before committing to any partnership that would be contractually difficult to get out of, consider carefully whether this is the best agent, editor, and publisher for you. You are the only one who can decide. If you are unsure, solicit some personal recommendations and referrals. Specifically, ask conference coordinators, editor/agent coordinators, folks on the conference committee, and published author friends. A good way to phrase the question is this: "If you were in my shoes, would you have any reservations about signing a contract with agent/editor Z"? Or "Would you highly recommend agent/editor Y or would you recommend I speak with more agents first?"

You can also check out the recommendations at Preditors & Editors (www.anotherealm.com/prededitors/pubagent.htm).

Visit the forum discussion at Absolute Write's Water Cooler (www.absolutewrite.com/forums). Read Bewares & Background Checks under the heading "Conference Room."

And for agents, check The Association of Authors' Representation at www.aar-online.org. If an agent is a member of this group, he should be reputable.

- What's the size of the potential market for this book? How could it be broadened or narrowed? What organizations exist for this market and how many members do they have?
- What indicators forecast a need for this book? (This includes blurbs from articles in national magazines and daily newspapers that relate to the topic.)
- What other books already exist on shelves that are similar to this book, yet not quite the same angle as this book? (Go to your local bookstore or check online retailers for ideas.)

Agents and editors are flying to a conference near you just to scout out talented writers to author books. If you'd like to be one of them, get yourself signed up to give as many pitches as you can with whichever agents and editors would be the most appropriate for your book concept. And if it looks like your book concept is too far afield, choose the agents and editors with the best reputations for offering career advice to conference attendees. A quick call to the conference's agent/editor coordinator will reveal your best choices.

So type up your three pages for your book concept, polish them, and become conversant on all of your key points. Because if you can treat your idea as a *concept* and not "your baby," chances are very good that you will walk out of a conference with everything you need to know to revise your book concept into a book proposal that will sell.

exercise

Prepare Your Book Concept With Others

Don't try to prepare a book concept for a conference by yourself. Not only is this more stress than any one mom needs, it's more fun to work on your book concept with others, and other people's input is key to your pitching success. In order to prepare your book concept (BC) for a writers conference, gather together a small group of Book Concept Advisors. Your Book Concept Advisors (BCAs) are writer-friends who help you prepare a viable book concept. Your BCA group can include:

- Potential readers of your book (friends, fellow writers, friends of friends)

- Published author friends who may be able to help you with your concept specifically, if it's similar to their book(s)

So if you have an idea for a book, start preparing that concept now. Find people who will be able to help you solidify your thoughts and create sales copy, a synopsis, and some market notes that you could present at a conference. If you are already part of a writing group, the other members may be the perfect place to start. But don't limit yourself. If there are other people who you think could help, don't hesitate to contact them. They may be honored that you thought of them and excited about helping formulate a book concept.

How to Pitch a Book Concept

A pitch is a pithy, punchy script that you memorize so that you can deliver it orally with confidence and ease. The key to a giving a successful verbal pitch—whether sitting in front of one agent or editor or standing in front of a panel of agents and editors (as at the Willamette Writers Conference)—is to write it short and practice it enough to memorize it.

When you finally deliver your pitch, you will do it, as my friend Elaura Niles likes to say, "as though you are a Miss America Contestant." No stuttering; no stammering; no "Uh, uh, uh … oh no, I forget!" Instead, deliver a well-rehearsed, catchy, and contagious few lines that make the listener nod and lean forward. *But don't talk longer than two minutes, please!* There is nothing worse than sitting in the crowd at a pre-conference panel pitch and listening to writers go on and on and on. (And then argue with the agents when they give them feedback!)

Here is an example pitch—it's the one I used to pitch this book:

Hi, I'm Christina Katz, a freelance writer for *The Oregonian* and mother of a toddler.

Three years ago I experienced the happiest moment of my life, followed by the most creativity-zapping, soul-sucking months from hell. I gave birth to my daughter, Samantha Rose, and my writing career, that I had spent years developing, disappeared into a black hole of diaper changes, marathon feedings, and sleep deprivation.

Since then I've learned how to balance motherhood and writing, publishing hundreds of articles in daily newspapers, periodicals, and online magazines.

Last year my piece on working moms was one of the most popular on the Web and resulted in an interview with Diane Sawyer on "Good Morning America."

I teach other moms how to do what I did and continue to do on a daily basis. My book proposal is titled "The Busy Mom's Guide to Freelance: 24 Steps to a Profitable, Part-Time Writing Career."

As you can see, the focus of the book has changed in the process of pitching it, negotiating it, and writing it. And you may be thinking that the pitch is rather dramatic for such a tame book as the one you are holding in your hands. But this is the whole point. A pitch draws attention to your book concept. How much attention and what kind of response people have to your idea is exactly why you've brought it to the conference to explore.

When they hear your pitch, agents and editors are assessing your idea, your delivery of your idea, and you. And you will be amazed at how they can do this just by hearing a one- or two-minute pitch. Like moms, whose intuition becomes very refined, agents and editors become good judges of book concepts. And if you hang around them long enough, you will become good at it too.

Afterword

There Is No End,
Just More to Learn

> *Money isn't that much of a motivator for me unless it's accompanied by self-satisfaction.*
>
> ~ C. HOPE CLARK, MOTHER OF TWO

Unlike many careers, you don't have to retire from writing upon reaching a certain age, or ever! A writing career can last as long as you like. In fact, the beauty of a writing career is that it will help your mind stay alert and healthy, both today and as you get older. So don't limit your writing career; just let it evolve as you evolve. Let it ebb and flow alongside your life circumstances. Let it grow alongside your kids!

Your children will always be your children, and your writing career will always be your writing career. When your kids leave for college, you can write about that. If they move to the other side of the world, you can write about that—or even better, go visit them and write about that! One of my mom students with a grown daughter did just that, and will soon have her essay published in *Transitions Abroad*.

Other moms I have taught write for national magazines, daily newspapers, online publications—you name it, they write for it. And they enjoy it. Some are being invited to submit their first book proposals. Now that's exciting! And this could be you someday, if that's what you want.

Think of the first year of your writing career as a grand experiment: Try some different possibilities before you narrow down your options. If a project grabs your attention, or you think you might gain good, solid professional experience, jump on it! If you try one specialty—say parenting articles—only to discover you don't enjoy writing them as much as you thought you would, you can always reassess and try again. That's the beauty of a freelance writing career. You always have options and you control the direction, so trust your instincts and choose!

Regardless of how you ultimately proceed in your writing career, remember that your answers to these four questions will ultimately make all the difference:

Is my idea appropriate?

Have I paid attention to the important details?

Am I acting like a professional?

And ... Did I follow-through?

The same ideas mentioned at the beginning of this book are still the most important! Why not apply them to what's on your writing goals list today?

For free resources for writer mamas and to learn how to connect with other writer mamas in your area, please visit www.thewritermama.com. Visit www.thewritermama.com and share your experiences with other writer mamas. You can also check out the Writer Mama blog and download free resources for writer mamas and writer mama circles.

I wish you the best of luck in all your writing endeavors!

Appendix
Recommended Reading

> I have not ceased to be fearful, but I have ceased to let fear control me. I have accepted fear as a part of life, specifically the fear of change, the fear of the unknown. I have gone ahead despite the pounding in the heart that says: Turn back, turn back; you'll die if you venture too far.
>
> ~ ERICA JONG, MOTHER OF ONE

The Complete Idiot's Guide to Publishing Magazine Articles, 4th Edition by Sheree Bykofsky and Jennifer Basye Sander goes into just the right amount of detail on topics like how to write a strong lede, which editor does what, and "the least you need to know" on a variety of topics, all while teaching you how to speak editorese. A solid freelancer primer.

Ready, Aim, Specialize, Create Your Own Writing Specialty and Make More Money by Kelly James Enger is a must-read if you think you want to specialize. Generalists can also learn helpful lessons to increase sales by incorporating the insight in this book. To be reissued by Marion Street Press in November 2007.

Starting Your Career as a Freelance Writer by Moira Anderson Allen is one of the most detailed books on the practical tasks facing freelance writers. You will pick up a lot of helpful ideas in this book for taming paper overload, backing up your work, and preparing for the taxman.

Beginning Writer's Answer Book, 30th Anniversary Edition, edited by Jane Friedman, is a good reference for those new to writing for publication. The book responds in a friendly tone to often asked questions about everything under a writer's sun: magazine and newspaper articles, nonfiction books, short fiction, poetry, scripts, and songs (and more).

The Writer's Digest Handbook of Magazine Article Writing, edited by Michelle Ruberg, gives tons of information about how to write different types of magazine articles. It also has in-depth information on submitting, querying, working with editors, and selling reprints and rewrites, and handling business issues. But if you aren't ready for all that, this book can also help you get started finding marketable ideas.

Another suggestion is to join Writer's Digest Book Club, which will continually introduce helpful books to you. Just as a gym membership makes you feel guilty when you don't use it, think of the Writer's Digest Book Club when you are ready to explore other genres. The membership commitment will push you to keep learning, even when you think you're too busy. Visit www.writers digestbookclub.com to join for free.

Index

A

AbsoluteWrite.com, 235

Accountability sheet, 199-200

Afternoon, finding time to write, 56-57

Agents, meeting at conferences, 259, 277-278

All rights, defined, 192-194

Allen, Moira Anderson, 196

The American Directory of Writer's Guidelines, 41, 43

American Society of Journalists and Authors, 197, 261

Anecdotes, 109-111

AP style, 148

Articles
  difficult situations when selling, 197-198
  fillers, 90-95
  how-to, 99-104
  list, 80-81, 83-86
  for opposite audiences, studying, 24
  personal essay, 108-115
  by staff vs. freelancer, 34-36
  terms of sale, 192-199
  See also Feature(s), Tips

Assignment
  defined, 148

landing, 167-169

Audience
  focusing on four, 22-24
  identifying, 20-25
  opposite, studying articles for, 24
  See also Market

Author readings, 140-141

Authors, meeting at conferences, 259, 261

B

B.O.B., defined, 31

Background, as specialty, 124, 126

Bailey, Maria, 248-249

Beginning Writer's Answer Book, 109

Bio, 62-63, 158, 276

Blogging, 13

Book. *See* Nonfiction book

Book Concept Advisors, 278-279

Bookkeeping and accounting, 218-223

Bookstores, cruising, 13

Boundaries, setting, 116-118

Buchanan, Andrea, 247-248

Burgett, Gordon, 196

Burnout, avoiding, 227-229

Burrell, Diana, 17, 37, 128, 151, 225

Burt, Wendy, 28, 122, 199, 255

Business cards, 269-270

Byline, defined, 31

C

Caller I.D., 122

Cameron, Julia, 107

Celine Dion: For Keeps, 235

Challenges, personal, as area of specialty, 124, 126

Childcare, 127-130

Child magazine, profile, 32

Christian Science Monitor, short essay in, 111-112

Cindrich, Sharon, 37, 82, 129, 168

Clark, C. Hope, 61, 95, 122, 169, 255-256

Classes, 4, 139-140
    online and e-mail, 152-153
    teaching, 254-255

Client service, focusing on, 176-177

Clips
    building portfolio, 48-54
    success with, 50

Closed-circulation publications, for getting clips, 51-52

Comfort Book series, 235-236

Computer, as workplace, 76-77

Conquering Panic and Anxiety Disorders, 235

Conscientiousness, 244

Consistency, 243

Consulting, as income source, 255

Content comparison sheet, 138, 147

Contracts, 193, 199

Contributor/contributing editor, defined, 31

Contributor's copies, defined, 148

Copyright, 193

Copywriting, as income source, 255

Cover letter(s)
    to accompany filler, 94
    demystified, 60-64
    formatting, 170-171
    proofreading, 63
    when to send, 59-60

Creative thinking, 241

Critic, finding helpful, 102

Custom publications, for getting clips, 51-52

D

Debt-Proof Living, 234

Departments, defined, 31

Description, as prewriting, 136

Detachment, 243

Determination, 241

Documents, important, saving and filing, 219-223

Draft checklist, 210-211

E

Editing, offering service, 255

Editor(s)
  connecting with, in cover letter, 60-61
  meeting at conferences, 259, 277-278
  points of view, 172, 225-226
  showing knowledge of publication to, 44
  working with, 175-177

Editorial calendar, 149-150

Editor-to-writer communication, in writer's guidelines, 42-43

Electronic address book, 122

Electronic rights, 194-195

E-mail
  having two accounts, 122
  querying by, 169, 171-173

Entertainment News Northwest, 53

Essays
  personal, 108-115
  short, 111-112

Evenings, finding time to write, 66-67

Evergreen, defined, 31

Expertise

building, 231-233
establishing and maintaining status, 238
identifying, 237
need for, 233
uncovering, 236, 240

Experts, finding, to interview, 180

E-zines, 153-154

F

F.O.B., defined, 31

Family Circle magazine, writer's guidelines, 42-43

Family Circle's 2000 Hints and Tips: For Cooking, Cleaning, Organizing, and Simplifying Your Life, 81

Family Fun, editorial calendar, 149-150

Faust, Julie, 276

Feature(s)
  prewriting, 133-137
  spinning fillers into, 94
  writing tips, 205-209

Feature well, defined, 31

Fictional devices, in essays, 113

Fillers, 90-95

Filters, 117-118

First rights, 194

Flexibility, of writing at home, 38

Follow-up, on submissions, 64

Foolscap & Quill's Writer's Pocket Tax Guide, 221, 223

Formatting & Submitting Your Manuscript, 170-171

Formichelli, Linda, 151, 255

Freelancer(s)
  list articles as markets for, 83
  roles, 223-225
  what not to write, 33-34

Freelancing
  benefits, 26-28
  identifying all opportunities, 33

Friedman, Jane, 109

Funds for Writers, 42, 95, 154

G

Generalist, defined, 120-121

Ghostwriting, as income source, 255

Glatzer, Jenna, 113-114, 235, 246, 255

Glossy regional publications, for getting clips, 53

Goals, setting, 201-203

Goldberg, Natalie, 241

Gore, Ariel, 247

Green, Abigail, 50, 52

H

Hard copy, defined, 148

Help, asking for, 116

Hobbies, as specialty, 125-126

Home office deduction, 223

Household management, streamlining, 96-98

How-to articles, 99-104

Hudock, Amy, 247-248

Hunt, Mary, 234-235, 246

I

Ideas
  making lists for, 15
  systems for organizing and keeping, 16-18

Income
  for article, 196
  developing multiple streams, 254-256

The International Women's Writing Guild, 260-261

Internet, connecting with other writers via, 5, 152-154

Interview(s)

asking sharp questions, 184

informational, 141-142

phone vs. e-mail vs. in-person, 181

practicing, 187

preparing for, 183

requesting, 181-182

role model, 106

short, 179, 181-187

See also Sources

Invoice, defined, 148

J

James-Enger, Kelly, 16, 37, 91, 93, 122-123, 254

Journaling, 11

K

Keywords, using to find audience, 21-25

Kill fee, defined, 148

L

Lamott, Ann, 17

Laufenberg, Cynthia, 170

Lede, 156-157, 206-209

Letter,
  as prewriting, 133-134
  See also Cover letter(s), Query letter(s)

List articles, 80-81, 83-86

Lists, and prewriting, 133

Local publications, for getting clips, 53

Louden, Jennifer, 235-236, 246, 255

Lyon, Elizabeth, 254

M

Magazines
  collecting, for potential audiences, 25
  national trade, for getting clips, 49, 51
  researching same-category, 30-31
  studying covers, 33
  terms, 31
  See also Zines

Mamas, publications by and for, 3

Manuscript evaluation, offering service, 254

Market(s)
  for essays, 114-115
  working with one at a time, 33

Market guide, defined, 31

Market research, 30-36
  for book concept, 276-278

Marketing, platforms, 246-253

Masthead
  defined, 31
  using for market research, 34-36

MediaBistro.com, 105

Media kit, defined, 31

Microsoft Office, 122

Mind-map method, 134

Mom Talk Radio, 249

MomWriters, 154

Morning, finding time to write in, 45-46

Mothering magazine, profile, 32

N

Name, company, dropping, 249

Negotiating, 192-199

Networking, 139-140
  informal, finding subjects and sources through, 188-190
  for sources, 185

The New Book of List: The Original Compendium of Curious Information, 81

Newspapers
  daily, for getting clips, 48-49
  for keeping up with

trends, 13
  local and regional, for getting clips, 54

Nonfiction book
  example of pitch, 280-281
  pitching at conference, 274-279
  proposals vs. concepts, 273-274
  writing, establishing expertise for, 231-240

Nonfiction book proposal, recommended reading, 274

Note-taking, vs. recording devices, 183

O

Ode, 13

Online market guides, 41

Online markets, for getting clips, 52

Online writing communities, 153-154

On-spec, defined, 148

Organizational tools and systems, 82, 206, 218-223

Organizations and associations, for finding expert interviews, 180

P

Paper, organizing, 82

Parenting magazine, 32-33

The Parents Book of Lists, 81

Parents magazine
  profile, 32
  tip categories, 71, 73

Partner, writing with, 130

Payment, typical, 196

Payment on acceptance, defined, 148

Payment on publication, defined, 148

Personal essay, 108-115

Personal experience, to make list articles universal, 85

Photos, providing, 54

Plagiarism, 146

Platforms
  defined, 246
  Q and A, 250-251
  samples, 247-249

Point of view, 135
  editor's, 172, 225-226

Poise, 7

Portfolio, building with clips, 48-54

Practice, 7

Preparation, 7
    for interview, 183
    for query letter, 144-145

Prewriting, 133-137
    and refreshing memory, 205

Prioritizing, 242

Problem/solution proposal, as prewriting, 136

Procrastination, 87-88

Professional Mission Statement, 121

Professionalism, 7
    ups and downs, 212-215
    when interacting with editors, 176

Profit-and-loss analysis, 220-221

Profnet, for finding expert interviews, 180

Prompts, 112

Proofreading, cover letters, 63

Publications
    collecting hard-to-find, 55
    custom and closed-circulation, 51-52
    glossy regional or local, 53
    matching with interests, 23-24

querying six at a time, 167
    See also Magazines, Newspapers, Nonfiction book, Zines

Public speaking, 254

Publishing, appropriate way to break into, 10

Q

Query letter(s), 144-147, 149-151, 156-174
    assessing best prospects, 147, 149
    checklist, 173-174
    e-mail vs. snail-mail, 169, 171-173
    formatting, 170-171
    gathering samples, 150-151
    samples, 158-166
    strong, 156-158
    terms, 148
    with time limits, 168
    writing, 149-150

Quotes
    getting best, 184-185
    in how-to articles, 101-102
    requests to "approve," 186

R

Reader's Digest, anecdotes in, 109

Reading materials, identifying audience through, 20-21

Ready, Aim, Specialize!: Create Your Own Writing Specialty and Make More Money, 122-123

Recording devices, vs. note-taking, 183

Redbook, editorial calendar, 150

Reprint rights, 194

Reprints
    defined, 148
    selling, 221

Research
    conducting quickly, 92-93
    for how-to article, 101-102
    list articles, 84
    market. *See* Market research
    See also Interviews

Resilience, 243

Rewrites, selling, 193

Rights, 193-195

Role models, finding, 105-107

Roles, personal, identifying audience through, 21-22

Routines, 117-118

Rusch, Elizabeth, 16, 37

S

Sales copy, for book concept, 275-276

SASE, defined, 148

Scene, creating, 137

"Scrap" documents, 209

Second rights, 194

Self-publishing, 255-256

Sell & Resell Your Magazine Articles, 196

Sensory description, as pre-writing, 136

Shaw Guides, 258

Shortridge, Jennie, 27

Shorts. *See* Fillers

Slant, defined, 148

Sources
expectations, 186
finding and interviewing, 179, 181
problems with, 185

Specialist, defined, 120

Specializing, 122-126

Starting Your Career as a Freelance Writer, 196

Stewart, Martha, 232

Style, defined, 148

Style manuals, 209

Submissions
keeping in circulation, 61
multiple, 73
three-step process, 64-65
unsolicited, 148
See also Cover letter(s)

The Sun, prompts in, 112

Sun Signs for Writers, 125

T

Table of contents, examining, 34

Talbott, Tiffany, 111

Target audience, 20

Taxes, 221-223

Television, for keeping up with trends, 14

Time, finding and protecting, 45-46, 56-57, 66-67, 116-117

Time limit, on query, 168

Timing, and fillers, 93-94

Tips
brainstorming ideas, 71-72
collecting, 81
list articles as, 83
multiple submissions, 73
stretching into lists, 86

writing and submitting, 70, 73, 75

Today's BlueSuitMom, 248-249

Topics
essay, 110
for how-to articles, 100-101
writing about favorite, 125-126

Trade magazines, for getting clips, 49, 51

Trends, tapping into, 12-14

U

Unsolicited manuscript, defined, 148

Utne Reader, 12

V

Voice, 101

W

Wallace, Amy, 81

Wallenchinsky, David, 81

Walton-Porter, Bev, 125

Web, connecting with other writers, 5, 152-154

Web site, publicizing, 249

Wilamette Writers, 260

Wooden Horse Database, 41, 43, 150

Work for hire, 195-196

Workplace, options, 76-78

Workshops, 4, 139-140
    meeting presenters, 261-262
    teaching, 254-255

Writer(s)
    connecting with others, 5, 139-142, 262-263
    interviewing other, 141-142
    sharing information about being, 117

The WriterMama Blog, 154

Writer Mama Circle
    creating group, 107
    regular playdates through, 130

Writer mamas, imitating attitudes, 241-244

Writers associations, 141, 260-261
    meeting members at conferences, 262

Writers conferences, 141, 258-267
    being prepared, 268-271
    getting jump on registration, 266-267
    pitching book at, 274-279
    reasons for attending, 263-265

Writer's guidelines, 40-42
    D.I.Y. strategies for finding, 42
    obtaining, 44
    for query letters, 169

Writer's Market, 151
    analyzing audience, 30, 36
    for writer's guidelines, 41, 43

WritersMarket.com, 41, 43, 95, 104

Writers on the Rise, 252-253, 255

Writing
    finding time for, 45-46, 56-57, 66-67
    for free, 71
    home-based, benefits, 37-38
    with kids underfoot, 129-130
    as response, 11-12
    skills for long essays, 112-114
    specializing in preferred form, 124-126
    ten reasons for, 3-6

Writing groups, 140
    See also Online writing communities, Writer Mama Circle

Y

Yellow Pages, for finding expert interviews, 180

Z

Zeitgeist, 12-14

Zines, 3

About the Author

Christina Katz trained as a writer at Columbia College, Chicago after earning a degree in English from Dartmouth College. She currently writes, co-parents her daughter, Samantha, and champions her teacher/director husband, Jason, just south of Portland, in Wilsonville, Oregon.

As a freelance journalist for such publications as *The Oregonian, Bluesuit mom.com,* and *Country Sampler,* Christina's byline has accompanied hundreds of articles, interviews, profiles, and columns over the past seven years.

Christina has appeared on *Good Morning America,* has mentored hundreds of nonfiction writers through her classes, and is publisher and editor of the popular online zine, *Writers on the Rise.*

A sought-after conference presenter and a monthly columnist on platform development for *The Willamette Writer,* Christina is a member of Willamette Writers and The International Women's Writing Guild.

When Christina isn't writing, she enjoys "family walks," chatting on the phone with friends and family, traveling around the globe, reading, eating out, taking road trips, building Web sites, attending cultural events, decorating, and making collages.

For more information, visit www.christinakatz.com, www.writersontherise.com, and www.thewritermama.com.